Beggars by W. H. Davies

William Henry Davies was born in the Pillgwenlly district of Newport, Monmouthshire, Wales, a busy port on July 3rd, 1871.

Davies seemed to find childhood difficult. By the age of 13 he was arrested, part of a gang of five schoolmates, and charged with stealing handbags. He was given twelve strokes of the birch. The following year, 1885, Davies wrote his first poem; "Death".

His yearning was to travel. In a half dozen years, he crossed the Atlantic at least annually by working on cattle ships. He travelled through many of the states, sometimes begging, sometimes taking seasonal work, but would often spend any savings on a drinking spree with a fellow traveller.

In London, he came across a newspaper story about the riches to be made in the Klondike and immediately set off to make his fortune in Canada. Attempting to jump a freight train at Renfrew, Ontario, on March 20th, 1899, he lost his footing and his right foot was crushed under the wheels of the train. The leg later had to be amputated below the knee and he wore a wooden prosthetic leg thereafter.

On October 12th, 1905 Davies met the poet Edward Thomas, then the literary critic for the Daily Chronicle. Thomas rented for Davies a nearby tiny two-roomed cottage. Thomas now adopted the role of protective guardian as he helped Davies to develop his career.

In 1907, the manuscript of The Autobiography of a Super-Tramp drew the attention of George Bernard Shaw, who agreed to write a preface.

In 1911, Davies was awarded a Civil List Pension of £50, which later increased to £100 and then to £150.

The Georgian poetry publisher Edward Marsh introduced him, in 1913, to DH Lawrence who was captivated by Davies and later invited him to Germany. Despite this early enthusiasm, Lawrence's opinion waned and he noted the newer verses seemed "so thin, one can hardly feel them".

On February 5th, 1923, Davies married 23-year-old Helen Matilda Payne, at the Registry Office in East Grinstead in Sussex. His book Young Emma chronicles the relationship in a very frank and revealing way. Having second thoughts he retrieved the book from the publishers and it was only published after Helens death. He had met her near Marble Arch decanting from a bus wearing a "saucy-looking little velvet cap with tassels". At the time Helen was unmarried and pregnant. While living with Davies in London, before their marriage, Helen suffered an almost fatal miscarriage.

Davies made over a dozen broadcasts for the BBC, reading his own work, between 1924 and 1940.

Davies returned to Newport, in September 1938, for the unveiling of a plaque in his honour, and with an address given by the Poet Laureate John Masefield. His health had now deteriorated, and this proved to be his last public appearance.

W. H. Davies' health continued to worsen and he died, on September 26th, 1940, at the age of 69.

Index of Contents

Chapter I

The Nationalities as Beggars

There is no question but that the American beggar is the finest in his country; but in that land of many nationalities he has a number of old-country beggars to contend with. Perhaps it would interest—it certainly should—a number of people to know how well or ill their own nation is represented by beggars in that most important country; whether England, Ireland, Scotland, Germany, and other countries have cause to be proud or ashamed of their representatives. Both France and Italy have much cause to complain, for you may often travel many miles and not be approached by a French or Italian beggar. If you meet an Italian, you can safely despise him as a working man with hard-earned money in his pocket, though he may be stealing rides like a beggar, and making coffee with real beggars at their camps.

With regard to Germany, she can place in the field a very large army of second-rate beggars; but it is seldom that you meet a German beggar whose ambition raises him above that. Other nationalities, who go to private houses and beg ready-cooked meals, despise the German beggar for his low taste in being satisfied with no more than common dry food. All beggars make coffee at camp-fires, but it is only the German that takes the trouble to carry on his travels his own tin can; for every town has near it a beggars' camp, and cans are always to be found. The German's method is to beg the baker for bread, the butcher for sausage, and the grocer for coffee. When he is successful, he repairs to the camp, and makes what he calls "an excellent meal" on these dry materials; whereas other beggars have either had a good hot meal at a private house, or have begged a number of paper parcels, in which is buttered bread, and there is cake, and one parcel may have fish as a change from the meat in another, and there is often an apple, orange, or banana for dessert. The German does not aspire to these luxuries, and is well satisfied to get the plain diet of his native land—without taking advantage of the offers of a richer country—and to do no work for it. He is not a true beggar either, for he is always ready to do odd jobs, such as fruit or hop picking and potato digging, but is not eager for steady work.

Few people would think the Scotsman makes an excellent beggar, seeing that his manner is so undemonstrative. Although he is seldom heard to raise his voice above one distinct pitch, or to indulge in loud laughter, or to show emotion of any kind, yet, for all this, he is an excellent beggar. There is quite a large clan of Scotties among American beggars. He is a good beggar for the simple reason that he is a good talker. Almost every Scotch beggar I met in the States of America was inclined to be talkative, and yet they all managed to conceal their private affairs. Although a Scotsman would be one of the last men to go hungry in a civilized land, yet he must be objected to as a true beggar in that he is avaricious for money, and would immediately take advantage of remunerative employment.

Alas for the poor Irishman! for he is the most timid beggar of all. Though he is so independent in throwing up a job, he is always glad, when his money is gone, to seek another. How the poor fellow does suffer hunger when seeking work, not having the courage to beg; and how independent and forgetful he is when his appetite is satisfied. Even the German, who as a beggar is despised by American, English, and Scotch beggars, stands head and shoulders above poor Pat. I am sorry to say so, but the truth of the matter is that Pat receives charity from other beggars—English, Scotch, and such American beggars as are proud of their Irish extraction. If these men do not feed him, they often show him a good house where he only has to show his face and be fed.

I remember a very mean trick being served on two Irishmen, Pat and Tim. The guilty one was a Cockney, and he was lucky to escape with his life. Seeing at the camp two hungry and helpless Irishmen, he promised to show them a good house, at which no beggars, however often they came, were refused food. The elated pair accompanied "Cockney" for this interesting purpose, and were soon shown a very large house, at which, the Cockney said, "he had been treated with as much consideration as though he were the Pope of Rome." He then left them to make their own arrangements, and, after much indecision, it was arranged that Pat should go first, and, on his return, his companion Tim should try his luck. Pat, with every confidence, approached the big house and rang the bell; but the door was almost immediately opened, as though the inmate had been lying in wait. The Irishman had scarcely opened his mouth when the man that answered the door shouted, "What, you big, able-bodied rascal? I'll give you something to eat," and rushed at the poor Irishman with a thick walking-stick. This was very serious, for Pat also saw the grinning face of a stalwart nigger behind his master, and the Irishman thought the best thing he could do was to leave in a hurry without more words, which he did.

It quite upset Pat to think that he had been induced to go first, so he made up his mind that Tim should share his misfortune. Therefore, when he returned and Tim asked, "What luck, Pat?" Pat rubbed his body, saying, "Begorra, there was more mate than five min could ate." On hearing this good news Tim braced himself and, after a long pause, walked with reckless determination towards the house. But Tim had no time to ring, for the door was suddenly flung open, and, before he could utter one word, a white man and a nigger began to attack him with sticks. Tim did not wait to argue or fight, but took to his heels at once. "This is a noice thrick, an' the both from Kilkenny," said he to Pat. "Spake out," said Pat innocently, although he had seen the whole transaction; "shure, we are frinds, and frinds should share and share aloike." I am very pleased to say that the two Irishmen had their reward when they returned, for three good American beggars had thoroughly worked the town, and had in their possession enough food for ten men—but the Cockney never returned to the camp. It was certainly a cruel joke to play on two hungry men, innocent and unsuspecting.

The English easily come next to Americans as beggars, especially when England is represented by the Cockney. He will often attain his ends after failing in a cross-examination and discovered in a lie; for his witty excuses and peculiar manner of expression are not to be resisted by Americans. Even the Irish-Americans, who are so bitter against Englishmen, make an exception of a Cockney, because of his witty talk and his disinclination to be serious. This impudence and command of speech have become proverbial among American beggars, and he is so much liked that I have seen men, who were about to leave a town, remain at a camp for two or three days longer, so as to enjoy the anecdotes and queer sayings of a Cockney that has just arrived. The Cockney—and he alone—is admired by those extraordinary beggars who are born Americans, and who are conceited enough to think that they could by their energies live well as beggars in the poorest slums in the cities of Europe. Aye, even the beggars of the Western States, who, owing to the great distances between towns, must never be without a dollar or two in their pockets—even these energetic beggars have great respect for a Cockney, though they scorn the petty food-begging operations of others.

I never in all my acquaintance with "Brum" saw him look so alarmed as when he entered a camp and saw a man making coffee, and near him was a pile consisting of a number of parcels of food. This man, who was a Cockney, confessed that he had just begged the town—and we soon had cause to know it, for I had great difficulty in getting one little sandwich, and though Brum brought to the camp enough for two, he must have had a great struggle, for he was away much longer than usual. That he had struggled hard was apparent from his behaviour, for in spite of the Cockney's friendly advances, Brum would hardly give him a civil word. Yes, there was not the least doubt but what Brum was jealous. Although we three remained in the camp together for two days, I could not help but notice that Brum would never allow the Cockney to get the start on him, but every time we went begging he quickly followed the other. And what do you think this Cockney had the impudence to say to Brum? "Old man," said he, "I'll see if I can beg you a pair of trousers." When he heard this Brum almost foamed at the mouth, for he prided himself on being one of the best beggars in America, whether it was in getting money, food, or clothes.

I know very little about the Welsh as beggars, as I have only met about half a dozen in America, and they were so timid that Wales had as little cause to be proud of them as Ireland of hers. I don't think Welshmen take kindly to begging, for, according to my later experience at home, half the beggars in Wales are Englishmen, though many of them can explain themselves in Welsh, having been in the country a considerable time. They certainly have good cause to remain there, for Wales runs America a good second in her generosity to beggars; as also does Ireland, but she is less able to give.

No doubt Russia, Spain, Greece, Japan, and other countries have their beggars by thousands at home, but they are ill represented in America. England has only Germany to fear, who has six beggars to England's one; but they have little energy and are badly trained, and one Cockney is equal to ten.

Chapter II

A Tramps' Camp in Texas

It has borne in upon me lately, with great force, that in those vagabond days at camp-fires in America I was enjoying life as it will never be enjoyed again. I was then in a land of plenty, where the people were so happy and good-natured that a bold beggar could often tell them straightforward that he would not work for ten dollars a day, which would cause more amusement than indignation, and he would still be assisted with the best of everything. In fact, the common necessaries of life were so easily to be obtained that a superior beggar like Brum had to show his superiority over the ordinary beggar like myself by begging out-of-the-way luxuries—such as cough lozenges and chewing-gum, and a clean shirt and socks once a week, while I washed mine in the woodland stream, and dried them at the camp-fire, or in the wind and sun. How often have I received unsolicited clothes and boots from houses at which I had simply asked for meals! But when I exposed such articles at the camp, before the eyes of other beggars, I always took the credit on myself for having begged them, for fear of Brum's scorn. At one house where I called, the lady wanted her garden cleared of fallen leaves, and offered me twenty-five cents and my breakfast to sweep the said leaves into a corner and set fire to them, which could be done in half an hour. I at once accepted her offer, although I was very much afraid that Brum or another would pass, and I would be received with scorn on my return to the camp. When I had done this task the lady gave me a good breakfast, with twenty-five cents placed at the side of my plate. After I had sat down to this meal the lady left the room and shortly returned with a pair of boots. I thanked her for her kindness, and she again left the room, and again returned, this time with a pair of trousers, a shirt, and a pair of socks. These things she wrapped in a large journal, saying that my soul would not be any the worse for reading that journal—which had a religious tendency. After leaving her I made separate bundles of these things, so as to pretend at the camp that I had received them at different houses, which would considerably enhance my reputation as a beggar, by showing my dogged determination to succeed. When I reached the camp I found that not only Brum had returned, but two others were there, namely, "Wingy," who had lost an arm, and "Frisco Fatty." I need scarcely say that when that pair of well-known beggars saw my success, they eyed me with great satisfaction and spoke with great respect, although they were too well bred as beggars to express any surprise. Of course, I made no reference to work, which would have caused Brum to blush with shame, and would most likely have made Wingy and

Frisco Fatty so disgusted that they would have left our fire and gone deeper into the woods, to make a fire of their own.

It was about ten o'clock, and we were sitting at the fire—Brum, Wingy, Frisco Fatty, and myself—all in the best of humours, each man having had a good breakfast. Brum now proposed that we should beg food for our pockets, at dinner-time, so that there would be no need to leave the camp for the rest of the day, and we could then make coffee and have our supper together. We had just agreed to this when into the camp walked a young fellow, not much more than a boy, who was picking his teeth. After saying, "Hallo, boys!" he continued to pick his teeth, and at last remarked, "The people in this town keep tough chicken, and I shall be mighty glad to be out of it." Saying this, he took hold of an old tin pot, turned it bottom uppermost, and seated himself next to Wingy. At the mention of chicken I noticed Brum's ears cock, and then an amused smile came into his face, but he made no remark.

Although the new-comer made anything but a favourable impression, he appeared nothing daunted, for there he sat, looking at the fire, and whistling, until such time as one of us would start a conversation. "I believe that I have seen your face before," said Wingy quietly, and looking the stranger full in the face. Now, Wingy knew that he had not seen him before, but he did not want his own presence disgraced by a new-made beggar—who is known to the profession by the name of "fresh cat." Therefore, if his thought had been truly expressed, it would have been, "Who are you?" The new-comer certainly answered Wingy's thought instead of his language, for he answered with great dignity, "I am Cincinnati Slim." As it happened that the city of Cincinnati was Wingy's winter quarters, and that he had never heard of or met this beggar there, you can imagine what a painful silence followed. However, although Wingy plainly showed by his expression that the camp was imposed on by the arrival of a "fresh cat," he soon recovered his good humour. But it was very fortunate that another fledgling beggar had not then arrived, or Wingy's Christian charity and forbearance would have gone up with the smoke of our camp-fire.

When dinner-time arrived we all left the camp, and each of us succeeded without much trouble in getting a hot dinner and extra cold food for supper. I was very fortunate in getting dinner at the first house I called at, and on going to another house was given a paper parcel, which contained two sandwiches and a banana; this I thought would be ample for my own supper, and returned to the camp. Now, my business could scarcely have been transacted quicker, and yet, when I arrived at the camp, I saw to my surprise Cincinnati Slim, picking his teeth. "Chicken again," he said to me, pulling a long face, as he struggled with his back teeth.

At last we were all together, and a very happy supper we had that evening. Cincinnati Slim had not arrived in the camp to hear our arrangements, so Brum, seeing more food than could be eaten, invited him to a share. Slim remonstrated, saying that he wanted nothing, having had an excellent dinner of chicken and sweet potatoes, and had not known of our arrangements, or he would have begged enough for a dozen men. Time after time I saw the same amused expression come into Brum's face as he watched Cincinnati Slim at supper, and I could not help but notice that the latter swallowed large mouthfuls of food with extraordinary speed.

The next morning Wingy proposed making a large stew, and each man was commissioned to beg certain articles after having had his breakfast. Cincinnati Slim was to beg bread, which was very easy; and I had to account for meat, which was quite as easy to obtain, seeing that it was very cheap in that part of the country. Wingy had the difficult task of begging coffee, sugar, pepper, and salt; and Brum's task to get raw vegetables was not to be envied. These arrangements left Frisco Fatty free, but he was too good a beggar to take advantage of this, and said emphatically that he would get a supply of tobacco. With these ideas we all sallied out.

On this expedition we all succeeded except Cincinnati Slim. He walked into the camp, after we had all returned, picking his teeth as usual. He complained that every time he asked for bread he was invited indoors to a hot meal, and that after this had occurred for the third time, he had been forced to give up in despair, for fear of another hot meal for an already overloaded stomach. However, that did not matter, for Brum had begged a loaf of bread, in addition to onions, potatoes, and tomatoes. He seemed to have expected the failure of bread.

At one o'clock the stew was ready, and we shared it out in tin cans, with which the camp was well supplied. Cincinnati Slim had an extraordinary appetite, and certainly ate twice as much as any other, and was encouraged by Brum to do so. He apologized for his third helping by saying that it was his favourite dish, and that it was a change from so much chicken. It was certainly a good meal, and we were all contented to remain in the camp for the rest of the day, with hot coffee and bread for supper.

When I awoke the next morning my companions were asleep, but Brum was not to be seen. After indulging in another nap, I awoke from my second sleep, and saw my companions washing and preparing to go for breakfast. I was just about to enquire for Brum when into the camp that true beggar walked. He, it seemed, had risen early, and begged his breakfast at a poor work-man's house—a deed that I had never known him to do before. At last we were all ready to seek breakfast, and Brum, having had his, was left smoking his pipe at the fire.

It was certainly a most extraordinary town for good-natured people, for in less than half an hour we were all back in the camp. "Where's Brum?" I asked Wingy. "I don't know," he answered. The words were hardly out of my mouth when Cincinnati Slim appeared, still picking his teeth, and close at his heels came Brum.

After Wingy and Frisco Fatty had left the camp, for they were on their way to Galveston, Brum looked straight at Cincinnati Slim and said, "Well, Slim, what kind of breakfast did you have? More chicken?" "Not this time," answered Slim; "ham and fried eggs." "You young liar!" cried Brum. "You have not been to a single house, for I have been following you all the time. You have had nothing to eat since you came except what you have had at this camp. If it were not for luck, young fools like you would starve. Here, take this"—and he threw Cincinnati Slim a paper of food. The latter sat down without a word and began to eat.

Chapter III

Daring Beggars

American beggars knock boldly at doors like kings' messengers. An imposing mansion with marble pillars is a challenge to them, and they dance up its steps and press the button of an electric bell with a violence that no familiar friends of the house would dare use; but an English beggar almost sinks into the earth when his ears receive the report of his timid hand. In fact, except in very rare instances, where a large house has been approached and—for a wonder—found good, and has become famous to the begging fraternity—except in these very rare instances, English beggars pass by large mansions as though they were empty churches or smallpox hospitals.

I don't suppose there is a more daring or more impudent rascal on earth than a good American beggar. It is always his boast that he has begged an ex-president, or the present one, and he claims to have received benefits from a number of well-known millionaires, actors, and prize-fighters. Such proud experiences never fall from the lips of an English beggar, for the simple reason that he lives on the working and middle classes. A row of small cottages is of more benefit to him than an equal number of fine villas, and he thinks that he is in a hungry wilderness when there is nothing to be seen but very large houses—and he is quite right.

It has always seemed strange to me that Americans, who as a race are notoriously eager to make money, should be so generous to a beggar. Even when they refuse it is often more on account of haste than meanness. Not only that, but they give with such indifference, and are never annoyed at being solicited, whether they are reading papers on the verandahs of hotels, or promenading a sea-beach in the company of ladies. And, what is more, they seldom pry into a beggar's past, except in such cases as when their interest is aroused by a beggar's speech. For instance, a gentleman's father or mother may have been English, Irish or Scotch, and when he thinks that he can detect that tongue in the speech of a beggar, he is very apt to ask one or two questions, and the beggar is invariably more generously assisted.

The American tramp begs in such a quick, thorough, business-like manner, with such calm persistence and with such confidence, that he must at last meet with success in the very worst places; for that reason he will not stand for cross-examination, and if people attempt to pry into his life, he is just as likely as not to tell them straight that he is a beggar, that he does not work, and never will.

The blindest housewife must soon have her eyes opened to the ingratitude of these men. Most of the houses in small American towns burn wood, so that a woman is often glad to give a tramp a good hot meal for five or ten minutes' wood-chopping. But when beggars are asked to chop wood for a meal, they complain of working on an empty stomach. Alas for their ingratitude! for, after being served with a good meal, they often walk away without a glance at the wood-pile. Some of them do worse—they take the axe, and after delivering one or two blows they manage to break the handle; then they take the axe to the mistress of the house, and after quietly apologizing for the accident, walk away with heavy bellies and light hearts.

One lady, who had been served this trick a number of times, had become so irritated, for she could no longer regard them as accidents, that she decided to feed no more tramps except when her husband was on the premises. Brum, my friend and tutor, unfortunately happened to call at this lady's house, and was at once informed that if he wanted a meal he would have to chop wood for it. Brum agreed to this, but suggested that he could work all the better for having the meal first. He was soon seated at the table, and after enjoying a very fine meal, repaired to the wood-pile. After chopping wood for five minutes he was just about to drop the axe and leave, when he heard a man cough. Looking in that direction, he saw to his surprise a man seated on a chair, watching him with a sarcastic smile on his face, and, what was far worse, a shot-gun was lying across his knees. There was nothing else for poor Brum to do than to continue chopping wood until the man gave him permission to go. Brum thought he would never regain his freedom, for it was a full half-hour before the man came forward and said, smiling coldly, "You may now go, for you have earned your meal."

For a long time after this incident the sight of a wood-pile made poor Brum feel faint and dizzy. No doubt it also filled him with a wish to have vengeance. It was a great pity that such a noble fellow should have to suffer this indignity through others. For Brum would always oblige the ladies by chopping a tiny bit of wood, but of course he would never work without first eating, and five minutes' work was his time limit for the very best of meals. He never broke an axe, or sneaked away without doing a little work.

Brum had his revenge when he took advantage of a lady at a large house, who was surrounded with servants of both sexes. This lady explained to Brum that she would give him a good meal, provided he would afterwards chop wood. He willingly gave a promise and took the meal. While he was chopping it came under his notice that his shoes were not altogether as good as they should be; so, after chopping enough wood to make a show, he deliberately chopped off the heel of his left shoe. After doing this he went to the lady and brought the "accident" to her notice. The result of this was that she, after looking in vain for an old pair, thought it cheaper to give Brum a dollar to buy a second-hand pair of shoes than to give away a pair of her husband's. So Brum was a dollar in pocket, for, being such a good beggar, he had very little difficulty in getting another pair, and of course people could see that he was sadly in need of them.

Ah, Brum was equal to almost any emergency, for he had marvellous impudence. See how he begged a dollar from the English consul in a seaport, and then went straight aboard a ship and begged soup of a common seaman! After which he swore that the soup had scalded his throat, and he begged sweetshops for jujubes to suck. A wonderful beggar! whose persuasive powers could succeed with a proud English consul, and was then equal to the task of approaching a common seaman.

But, after all is said, the most daring feat that was ever performed by an American tramp is not to be put to the credit of men who have begged presidents, millionaires, and consuls, but to a dirty, unkempt, hairy tramp, whose mind was suddenly illumined by the light of divine genius.

This man was so dirty and ragged that he was a disgrace to third-rate beggars, much less such men as Brum, New Haven Baldy, and Detroit Fatty. This man, satisfied with rags, dirt, and long matted hair and beard, suddenly became ambitious for fame, and inspired with an idea that had never before entered the minds of the most daring tramps. After having slept in the open air for a number of months, this man not only determined to sleep in a bed, but to wake the next morning famous like Byron. Inspired with this noble idea, he journeyed to a distant town, where lived the richest man in the land, surrounded by luxuries unequalled by kings. Everything was in the tramp's favour, for the richest man in the land was away from home, and the poorest and dirtiest man in the land had decided to sleep in the former's bed! That this tramp was under supernatural influence there can be no doubt, or how could he enter the grounds, much less the house, without being seen by one of the numerous servants? Again, what led his feet direct to that room—one of a hundred—and whispered in his ear, "This is his bed"? And such a bed it was! so white, so soft, so comfortable, that the happy tramp slept long after daylight.

No doubt he would have slept much longer, had he not been disturbed. For when next morning a servant entered the room, she saw, to her surprise and horror, some very ragged clothes at the foot of the bed, and a black tin can, which the tramp used for making coffee, hanging on the beautiful bedpost. After which she saw a very dirty pair of hands on the bed, and then she shrieked, for she now saw the dirtiest and roughest-looking face she had ever seen, there, on her master's white pillow. Her startled cry soon brought others, and it was not long before the sleeper, now awake and smiling, was out of bed and standing between two indignant constables, who stared at the dark shadow of their prisoner's head on the white pillow.

This, I believe, was the most daring feat that was ever performed by a tramp.

Chapter IV

Dilemmas of Travellers

However careful a tramp may be to avoid places where there is abundant work, he cannot always succeed. It was in a small town in Texas that I had such a narrow escape of losing the delightful companionship of Brum. I had gone to a sawmill boarding-house in expectation of getting a good free dinner, having taken the precaution to wait until all the men had returned to work, so that I would then see no other than the lady of the house, and she, of course, would know little about work at the mill. When I knocked, the lady answered the door, and after hearing my story invited me indoors. She was a fine, motherly-looking woman, stout—the very kind of creature in whom Brum had so much confidence, that she herself lived well, and would sympathize with others that could not do the same. But who should I see when I got inside but the manager or owner of the mill, who, for some reason, had not yet returned to business. As a general rule a woman is trustful, and will believe almost anything; but I was now unexpectedly confronted by a hard business man, who would probably ask a number of awkward questions of trades that maybe he knew something about. While I was having dinner, these questions were put to me and apparently answered to his satisfaction. "Now," said he, when I was preparing to leave, "I can find you work at the mill, and you can start at once. I am not reckoned to be a bad master; the wages will certainly not be bad for a beginner, and you will never, I am sure, have cause to complain of this boarding-house. Your face appears to be open and honest, and you have a straightforward look that I like." The last remark made my face as red as a beetroot with guilt, which he, no doubt, took to be a pleasant sign of modesty. This was a most awkward position, and I began to explain myself. "Sir," said I, "I am a tailor by trade, and am now on my way to Houston, where I am sure of getting work. I earn three, four, and sometimes five dollars a day at my trade, and am the main support of a family of little sisters and brothers. So you see how others must suffer if I accept work in a mill at a dollar and a quarter a day. Not of myself I think, but others." The man seemed to be quite satisfied with this explanation, and said, "At any rate, you shall have a little job and earn a dollar to help you on the way." Then turning to the landlady, he asked the following question, which almost froze the marrow in my bones: "Where is that dark pair of trousers that were split?" As the reader will guess, I was no tailor, and could do no more than sew a button on a pair of trousers. So what a sigh of relief I gave when the kind-hearted woman said that she had given them away some time before. The man was now thoughtful, and I was very much afraid that he was trying to bring to mind other wearing apparel that would need repair. Being afraid of this, I rose, and hastily thanking them for my good dinner, walked towards the door. He followed me, being on his way to the mill, and before I left him he placed in my hand a silver half-dollar, wishing me good-bye and good luck.

Brum was very pleased to see me coming, as he had begun to have fears that I had been arrested, or had been offered work and accepted it. Brum was very particular as to what kind of companions he made, and if he lost me he might have travelled alone for a considerable time.

Some time after this Brum and I were very awkwardly placed when a party of boys determined, in pity for our idleness, to find us work. These boys were squirrel-shooting in the woods, and seeing our camp-fire at once came forward and began a sociable conversation. All the boys were armed with guns, and that is the reason why boys in that part of the world are not in much fear of tramps, in fact the fear is more likely to be on the tramps' side. Now it happened that some railroad work was being done close to our camp, and the work was in the hands of Italians. The boys, having probably heard their elders speak ill of such people, determined that we two idle Americans—judging by our language—should be installed in the place of the Italians, and the latter driven out of that part of the country. "Come!" they said to Brum and me, "we will soon find you work." This was very awkward indeed, and poor old Brum began to totter in the camp and groan. "What's the matter?" asked one of the kind-hearted lads. "Boys," said Brum slowly, and with great difficulty, "I am a very sick man. I am now making my way to Houston as fast as I can, to get hospital treatment." "Yes," I said firmly, and with quick apprehension. "Yes, and it shall never be said that I deserted a sick companion." "Good luck to you," said one of the lads, after which they soon left.

There was no other course now than to leave this place at once, for if we stayed any longer we were certain to see one of these lads again, seeing that there were so many of them and that the town was very small.

In spite of this disinclination to work, there are times when a tramp feels inclined to break the monotony by doing a little light labour. With such a noble resolve Brum and I left Houston to pick strawberries on our way to Galveston. On reaching the land of strawberries, we immediately made enquiries as to the prospect of work, and were recommended to a large farm which was under the control of a syndicate of Chinamen. On approaching the boss Chinaman and explaining our wish, we were at once engaged. At this farm each Chinaman seemed to be allotted one task. One was to be seen with a large watering-can watering the plants from morning till night, in sunshine or rain.

The next morning we started to pick after having received our instructions from the boss Chinaman, namely, "To pickee clean, and leave a little stem so as people can catchee hold of the bellies." Alas! the difficulty was to find the berries, and we were to be paid according to our picking; the water-carrier was far too industrious, for his watering beneath a hot sun was certainly bad for the plants; it did not require a farmer to know that. Needless to say, we remonstrated in a very short time and demanded our wages, in spite of the boss Chinaman coming forward with three berries on the palm of his right hand, and crying exultingly, "Lookee at the big bellies I pickee!"

We received our money, which amounted to very little, less than half a dollar between us, and left. It is surprising the number of jobs that I have left with very low wages to come, just enough to buy a bag of peanuts or the price of a shave.

Of course we would not have been quite so independent as this had we not left Pat Healey at work two weeks before.

Thinking he must now have ten or fifteen dollars saved, we resolved to call on him, and after getting him discharged, help him to spend his savings. With this object we boarded a fast freight train, and arrived that night at the place where we had left him—where he had accepted light work in a garden.

The next morning Brum called at the house for breakfast, which the good lady at once supplied. Brum had not seen any signs of Pat, so he made enquiries, and the lady informed him that the man had gone away the day before, "with ten or fifteen dollars," thought Brum, and groaned.

I was so disappointed when I received from Brum this information, that I was ill for several days after. I must have been light-headed for several days, for I thought every voice I heard was Pat calling to us, and every form I saw in the distance seemed to be his.

Chapter V

Queer Places

The most annoying position I was ever in was when travelling afoot in the State of Tennessee. There were three of us together, and two had money in plenty—that is we had enough to supply ourselves with the necessaries of life for a month at least. But we had made the great mistake of leaving the railroad, on which the towns were built, and walking the back country roads, which were wild and unfrequented, with a stray house here and there. The mistake was that we had not taken the precaution to supply ourselves with provisions, not doubting but that with money we could purchase food at any house which we might chance upon. We had passed several houses and, at last, beginning to feel the pangs of hunger, made up our minds to call at the next house we came to. Three houses passed, and we had not seen one that was likely to serve our purpose—no houses except negro shanties and a planter's large house lying far back from the road. When we did at last come to a decent-looking place, we were by then three hungry and desperate men, and were not long in explaining to its owner the object of our visit. On our appearance that gentleman seemed none too pleased, and, in spite of our confession of hunger, and our willingness to pay to have it appeased, did not seem in any way to favour our presence. He was outside the house when we accosted him, and, after hearing us and refusing further conversation, began to make his way indoors. We knew, of course, that once inside he would take more drastic measures to get rid of us, that he would arm himself and order us to be gone. Knowing this, Texas Jack at once drew a revolver and made him stand, while we lost no time in going indoors and helping ourselves, taking as much bread and bacon as would do for a meal. Before we left the house, my companion hid the farmer's gun, which we saw standing in the corner. We then told the farmer what we had done, and after advising him not to follow us, and giving him a dollar bill—which was four times the worth of what we had taken—made our way along the road as fast as we could. No doubt the man had been afraid we would not pay him, and we knew well that he was hardly likely to follow us after receiving a dollar for such a small theft.

But it is in the backwoods of Arkansas where the most unenlightened people of America live. At one time I was walking a railroad in that State, which for a number of miles was little more than trestles built over the swamps. There was very little solid foundation, although for years men had been filling in the deep hollows under the rails. In my ten miles' walk I saw a hundred snakes sunning themselves on the track. They would crawl out of the adjoining swamps and lie between the sleepers, many of them cut in two, having been caught by a train when they were lying across the rails. These snakes were all dangerous to tread on, and it was necessary for a man to keep his eyes continually on the earth, and to stand still if he wanted to look elsewhere.

There is one very interesting creature in the swamps of Arkansas, and that is the wild hog, who has made himself famous under the name of "Razor-back." Four of us had made our camp in the driest place we could find near the track. We had carried with us from the last town a quantity of bread and bacon, a tin of tomatoes, and a few ears of green corn. Scarcely had we settled to our meal when we heard grunting, and were soon surrounded by a score of these wild, half-famished hogs. We had cooked the corn, and after picking the cobs had thrown the latter into the hot ashes. At last these hogs became so bold and desperate, after having been repeatedly driven away, that they began to poke their snouts into the hot ashes for the burning cobs of corn. Of course they severely burned their poor snouts, and grunted in great pain, but they did not leave a single cob to be destroyed by fire. The empty tomato can fell to the lot of the greediest hog. He, trying to get at the bottom, made such a desperate attempt that the can fastened on his snout, and he at once hurried off into the back swamps, muzzled it seemed for life.

It was on this occasion that I happened to see one of these wild hogs running in front of a fast-approaching train. He had been crossing the track, when he suddenly heard the whistle of an engine. Turning his head, he saw to his consternation that some huge thing was rushing upon him, and was increasing in bulk as it came. Instead of leaving the track the hog gave a grunt and ran, with his enemy in pursuit. Making a stop, and again looking, he saw his enemy close upon him, and, giving one more grunt, louder this time, ran for his life. Alas! that was his last run on earth, for, just as he was about to turn and face the iron monster for the third time, the latter struck poor Mr. Hog and tossed him some twenty or thirty feet in the air, after which he fell lifeless in the swamp. His fellow-hogs made much of his death, and after grunting a few rapid prayers, soon had their unfortunate brother buried—in themselves.

The very few natives that inhabit these swamps get their principal meat supply from these hogs. They generally manage to grow enough corn to provide them with bread, so they live from one year's end to another on a monotonous diet of cornbread and hog's meat, or, as it is said, "corn dodger and sour belly." They are very lazy and indifferent to money, and life in these swamps suits them well. Newspapers and books they know little of, and it is said in other parts of the Union: "The people of Arkansas don't know the war is over," meaning, of course, their own civil war between North and South. They manage to keep themselves in boots, clothes, ammunition, coffee, and chewing tobacco, by bartering a few skins. The Americans did not get their name of hustlers from Arkansas. In some parts of this state, where the swamp lies near the Mississippi, and is therefore liable to be flooded at any time, the natives build their little wooden houses on piles driven deep into the soft earth. These houses look more like large pigeon-coops than human habitations, and to enter the front door it is necessary to climb a steep ladder. It is certainly lucky that poverty and distance from towns force these people to be teetotallers, or half of them would often have to sleep under their houses instead of in them. Of course, all Arkansas is not like this, for there are a number of fine towns in the state, and the people in those towns are as far advanced as in any other town of the Union; but the truth must be told, that Arkansas is the last place in the world to recover from the Great Flood; and that she still persists in remaining in a damp condition, to breed snakes and deadly flies, in spite of the efforts of her inhabitants to make things otherwise. She is still in a condition to breed fever, and her inhabitants are thin, and their skin is hard and leathery.

When I enquired of a native the distance to the next town he didn't know. I asked him if it was two miles—he stared. I asked him if it was fifty miles, but he still stared. It seemed that the poor fellow did not understand mileage, so I asked how long it would take to walk there. "Yer'll have to be right smart to get there by sundown," said he. I then asked him the size of the town, but this he did not know, for he had never been there, but came very near going there a year ago. I then asked him if he knew anyone that had been there, and he answered that "Ole man Johnson was there the fall before last." What was Johnson's opinion of the town? "Right smart," said my man.

Of course I did not expect to find a town like London, New York, or Chicago, or even a town with tramcars, but I must confess to disappointment when I found nothing but a store, a railway station, and five or six miserable-looking houses.

Another time I met a native of this same State of Arkansas, who was well dressed, and seemed to be more intelligent than others. In the course of conversation he asked me where I came from, and on being told that I came from England, he said, "You are a long way from home." The man certainly spoke with more culture than I had expected, and it filled me with astonishment when he requested me, in English better than my own, to say something to him in my own language for his amusement.

Chapter VI

Stiffs

In England the poorer classes often refer to a corpse as a "stiff un," and naturally one would suppose that the word "stiff," used as a noun, would mean the same. But in America the noun stiff is not applied to dead people, but as a term of scorn for hard-working men and others. For instance, one is called a "shovel stiff," another a "cattle stiff"; then there is the "mission stiff," and the "barrel-house stiff." Shovel stiff is the name applied by tramps to navvies and railroad workers. If one of the latter enters a tramps' camp, being out of work and looking for it, it is not long before he sees that his presence is not wanted. He is generally known by his clothes or his heavy boots. Tramps wear light boots, which are begged at the better class of houses, the inmates of which do not wear heavy boots. So when a man on tramp is seen to have on a heavy working pair, it can reasonably be supposed that he has bought them, and must have worked to enable him to do so. For this reason he is only a tramp for the time being, and is despised for being a shovel stiff. Even if his clothes or boots do not betray him, he is not long in the camp before he is found out, for he begins to question Baltimore Fatty, Boston Slim, or Frisco Shorty, and others, as to the prospect of getting work in certain places. Some of these free spirits answer him politely enough, saying, "We don't know, Jack." A shovel stiff has no other name than Jack, not considered being worthy of the name of "New York" Jack, "Chicago" Jack, or any other name of a city that should be proud to own him. "We don't know, Jack," they answer, with some dignity; "we never work." Others lose patience at once and say, "We don't want to be bothered in this camp by a gol darn shovel stiff."

My friend Brum was a tramp of the best, but he had too much pity for working men, and was too kind-hearted to openly insult the poor shovel stiff. But he confessed that the worst night he ever spent was at a fire with one other, who turned out to be a shovel stiff. Brum said that the poor fellow was building bridges, making railroads, and digging canals all night, until he had to be told sternly to stop and go to sleep. He never seemed to get tired of talking of work, and Brum had to at last address him like this: "Look here, old fellow; last night you cut a tunnel right through the Rocky Mountains, and you also bridged the Mississippi, where it was a mile wide; in addition to these you dug a canal from Chicago to New Orleans, nearly a thousand miles, and a number of smaller jobs, which were difficult, but which we will not mention; now, after doing so much work in one night—arn't you tired?" Of course, as can be expected, Brum did not travel far with such an industrious companion.

A cattle stiff is another term of reproach, used by sailors, firemen, and boss cattlemen, towards the men who do the heavy, dirty, and ill-paid work. I was a stiff, and no more, when I received two pounds for a trip, and all the other cattlemen—except the foreman and two men with first-class experience—received only ten shillings each. Being the best-paid stiff on board, I was made night watchman, which really means that for the whole night I was alone in charge of the cattle—being foreman, experienced man, and stiff, all in one. On the second night out, I happened to be forward inspecting the cattle, when I suddenly heard a fierce shout from the bridge. I took little notice of this until I heard a second shout, and could not fail to hear the words, "Cover that light!" Of course, I never dreamed that the order was meant for me, seeing that I had nothing to do with the working of the ship, my whole duty being with the cattle. Taking no notice, I proceeded about my work, swinging the lantern here and there; but in less than a minute I heard another fierce shout, and immediately after I was standing face to face with the first mate, he—a man very much disliked on board ship—standing before me in a great rage. "You dam stiff!" he shouted; "didn't I tell you to cover that light?" "What have you got to do with the light?" I demanded, angered at the word stiff. "You look after the ship, that is your work; mine is with the cattle." He grew almost mad with rage, and I believe, if he had not seen the axe—which the night watchman carries in his belt in readiness for wedging loose boards, etc.—if he had not seen that axe, there is no doubt but that he would have resorted to violence. As it was, he ran up the deck shouting that he would have me put in irons. It happened that the cattle foreman had not yet gone to bed, and, hearing the fierce shouts of the first mate, left his room to know the cause. To him the first mate hastened to explain, saying that he had been dazzled by my lantern, and that he had become so confused as to take it for another ship, and that if I did not obey his orders to keep the light covered on one side, he would have me put in irons. It never once occurred to me that the safety of the cattle was one with the safety of the ship, and I answered that I had signed no articles to obey captain, first mate, or any other officer, and that the ship could burn or sink, but my duty was still confined to the cattle. However, I promised to do my best not to blind the look-out by swinging my lantern, but what aggravated me most was to be called a stiff.

Then there is the mission stiff. This man is also despised by Baltimore Fatty and his ilk. He is certainly a beggar, but he concentrates his mind in one direction, and if he was in any place where there was no mission-room he would be likely to starve. Most of the mission-rooms supply soup and bread during the winter months, and it is at such places that this class of stiff is to be found. He waylays members of the choir and the respectable people that attend the mission, and from these he not only gets tickets for soup, but invitations to their houses, where he receives clothes and performs a little labour for money. He attains this end by attending the mission and giving a short testimony relating the change of his soul from black to white. The mission stiff is greatly despised, for he talks of nothing else, and he knows and has worked every mission in the country. I have been called a shovel stiff, a cattle stiff, and a barrel-house stiff, but have never been called a mission stiff, although I have mixed with them.

The sole occupation of a barrel-house stiff is to stand outside public-houses waiting for invitations to drink. He speaks familiarly to all men that approach, and some of them say, "Going to have one?" On which he replies, "Yes." When he is once at the bar, he seldom leaves it till the house closes at night. There is not often more than one or two barrel stiffs to one house, and that is why the landlord welcomes them; in fact he often invites the stiff to have a drink, and sends him on an errand or uses his services to collect empty glasses. A barrel-house stiff is the most despised of all stiffs, for the simple reason that he is a physical wreck and, though a swaggerer and a loud talker, is as powerless in action as a babe. He has no wind and his appearance is false, being red and fleshy. He lives on beer, and when he helps himself to the free lunch on the counter, he eats little more than a bird. He does not eat that little with appetite and relish, but takes his food as a medicine that must be taken in small quantities. The barrel-house stiff is the shortest liver of all stiffs, and the shovel stiff is after all the noblest and least deserving of reproach.

Chapter VII

American Prisons

Most people have heard that American prisons are not so hard as those of other countries, and they think of them as hotels for comfort, where a man loses nothing but his liberty. This is quite true of the North, but some of the Southern States can tell a different story. In England all prisons are much the same, but those of America not only differ in the various States, but even in the adjoining counties of the same State.

When I travelled Connecticut and Massachusetts in winter it was very pleasant, night after night, to be lodged in a warm room. All we had to do, after we had begged the town, was to call at the police station, where the officer in charge would take our names and occupation. Sometimes we were searched, and knives and razors taken from us, to be returned on the following morning; but the police would not make any comment on the food in our pockets. After this we were conducted to a large clean room, heated by steam; and there we could eat, smoke, and chat with happiness, until sleep overpowered us. The next morning we were at liberty to go our way, without a question of performing some task for our accommodation. In some cases we were even given a drink of hot coffee, with a piece of sausage and bread. Of course, good beggars would firmly but civilly decline these, for they could beg a better breakfast at a private house, and they would not spoil their appetite. Some of them, being very good beggars indeed, would tell the officer this; while others, more kind and considerate, would take what was offered and give it to some poor shovel stiff (navvy) out of work, or a fresh cat (new beginner). You must not be surprised at good beggars taking the accommodation offered by a police station, for common lodging-houses are not known in America, except in large cities.

The following incident will prove how jails differ even within a few miles of each other. I and another had been treated well, night after night, in the various police stations of Connecticut and Massachusetts, and one night we came to a nice little town in the latter State. We had not the least difficulty in begging supper. In fact we hardly parted, for my companion was invited into the first house he called at, and the same thing happened to me at the house next door. It was a very strange, neat piece of business; for we were both standing together at different doors, and even chatted while we waited; and the both doors were answered at the same time; and, at the same time as a man's voice said to him, "Come in," so a woman's voice said the same words to me. We could hear one another's steps going to the supper table, and our movements could be heard so plain that one must be aware when the other was leaving the house.

My companion was an American and a fast eater, and I heard them letting him out when I was about three parts through with my supper. However, he waited and, when I rejoined him, we both sought the police station, not dreaming but what it would be like the others visited on the previous nights. Being strangers in that town, we were at a loss which way to turn. Therefore, when I saw a boy coming near, I enquired of him as to where the marshal was to be found. Seeing him look astonished, I rewarded his curiosity by telling him our business—that we wanted a night's lodging at the police station. "What!" he cried in amazement; "what: not in the cooler?" I was quite surprised to hear this word "cooler," for I had never heard it before. However, just then the marshal came and, after hearing our wants, said, "Certainly, boys, follow me." He then led the way down a dark side street and in a few minutes stood before a small stone building, with one storey, and one room—to all appearance—and with bars at the window. Taking from his pocket a large key, he opened the door and walked in, inviting us to follow him. When we were all three inside, he struck a match, and by its light motioned towards a dark corner, saying, "You will find blankets there, boys; make yourselves comfortable." He had scarcely uttered these words when the light went out—and so did he; for, before we could ask one question, we heard the key turned in the lock, and we were left alone. My companion shouted several questions after him, but he did not answer or return. We wanted to know several things, the principal one being about drinking water.

By the light of a match, which I held, my companion found the blankets—two dirty, ill-smelling, thin blankets, and half a one. Here was a difference in treatment. Twelve miles from this place we were treated better, some people would think, than we deserved, but this was downright cruelty.

Ah! well I remembered the boy saying "cooler"! For it was the dead of winter, and the floor was of stone, and we only had two thin blankets and a half between us. The place was also very damp, for no fire had ever been lit in this building. I need hardly say that we had to run about all night in the dark to keep our bodies from freezing, in spite of being good beggars and well-fed men.

There is so much difference in the prisons of America that tramps always—when they incline for a change, thieving instead of begging—discuss at the camps the accommodation of the prisons that await unsuccessful attempts. The kind of thieving tramps mostly go in for is breaking seals and robbing cars of their merchandise; and the time of year they do these things is on the approach of winter; so that they may either be in a good warm jail during the cold months, or else have freedom with plenty of money in their pockets.

I knew one good jail, in Michigan, that was very hard to break into. A man could beg with impunity at private houses or in the public streets without being arrested, and tramps had to resort to other methods to attain their ends. They would go boldly and take things from the doorways of shops, and would then, to their delight, be arrested, charged with petty larceny, and sentenced to from twenty to sixty days. They did not snatch the things and run, but deliberately took them under people's eyes. When they were in their much-coveted jail, they had nothing to do but play cards, smoke, read, eat and sleep.

There was some difference between that place and the Old Prison at New Orleans. When I was arrested there, with six others, for sleeping in a freight car, we were all sentenced to thirty days. The judge—an old Southerner, who could never forgive the North for freeing the slaves without giving their owners some compensation—this old judge commented very severely and bitterly on our coming South, to live on its charity, instead of staying where we belonged. "We don't want you down here," he said; "but now that you are here, we will keep you for a time."

Only niggers and the poorest white people were sent to this Old Prison, for there was a new place for the better-class prisoners. Indeed as there were no clothes supplied, there could not be any mistake as to the class of prisoners. No such a thing as a bath, no work, and no discipline. At night we were lodged in large cells that had a number of bunks in each, and we could not sleep for the cold. In the day we walked about in a large yard, several hundred prisoners. Some of the new prisoners, not yet tamed by cold and hunger, would laugh, sing, and dance, and fights were not unusual. Our food consisted of a small quantity of bread and some greasy water, almost starvation. The men that had been confined there for a month or more were like skeletons. The object seemed to be to keep us alive, and no more, so as to save the expense of burying us. A number of prisoners had gone simple of mind. There was one—a Chinaman—and no one seemed to know how long he had been there or what for, as he could not speak a word of English. I often think of the poor wretch—the most pathetic figure I have ever seen. When he was walking up and down the yard, he would suddenly come to a standstill and, in a very clear, high voice sing his grief like a bird. Every prisoner would be startled by this sudden and unexpected wail, and a dead silence would come, which before was all buzz. But, as can be expected, this effect would not last long, for some simple prisoner, as mad as the Chinaman himself, would begin to shout and laugh, and others would soon join him. Then the poor Chinaman would stop and, wrapping his loose garment about him, begin again his silent walk to and fro. In an hour or two after, the place would be again startled by that high, clear voice, and the same silence would come, and the same jeering would break the spell.

While I was in this prison we had a fall of snow—which is exceptional in that part—and we suffered very much on that account. But the snow was very kind to the mad Chinaman, for he was found dead the next morning, with snow on his body. And yet he was in a cell—but I am not prepared to enter into a description as to how this prison was arranged. All I know is that I saw the cell with the door open and the dead man's feet just inside, covered with snow. No doubt the governor gave a satisfactory account of the prisoner under his charge.

Chapter VIII

Experiences of Others

Some of my experiences may sound a little exciting to men that have led a quiet life at home, but I would not care to mention them in the hearing of some men that I have met. One of my worst experiences was in riding the rods of a train, in the State of Texas, on a road that was notoriously hard to beat. Riding the rods means to stretch one's body under a car, on a narrow board four inches wide, which is fastened to two thin iron rods. Tramps never ride in this way, except when the brakesmen are very bad and would strike them off the bumpers, and there is not one unsealed, empty car on the train. But when a tramp is safely on the rods, and the train is going, it is then impossible to reach him with anything until the train stops. Of course if the rods broke, or anything happened to the board, or the tramp went to sleep, he must then fall and be cut to pieces. All these freight trains have rods, but a great number are without boards; for that reason a tramp often gets his own board and drives a nail into each end. When the train begins to move he throws his board across the rods, and then leaps under the car. His life now depends on the nails keeping in their place, the board not breaking, and keeping awake. But sometimes, unfortunately for the tramp, the brakesmen see a train out; which means that they will stand one on each side of the train, at the head of the engine, and inspect each side of the train as it passes them. If they see a tramp on the top of a car, or on the bumpers, they shout to him to get off, and, when they have themselves boarded the train, they come back over the top to see whether he has obeyed them or not. It would be wise for the tramp to do so, for the train would then be going slow; but if he does not, these brakesmen will force him after, at the point of a revolver, to jump off a train now going fast. But if they see a tramp on the rods, they are in a strange position. It is no use to tell him to get off, because he cannot do so until the train stops; and, as they cannot reach him, he rides in spite of them. They can only do one thing, and that is what I, and many more, have had done, and it is not a pleasant experience. These brakesmen arm themselves with stones, and one of them no sooner sees a tramp under the car than he shouts to his fellow. After doing this the two brakesmen run with the train, throwing stones with all their might, and the tramp can hear their savage yells and the stones strike against the car. As it is, he is in a shaky position, without being helped to fall by receiving a blow on the head with a stone. Fortunately for him, they must soon stop throwing, for the train is going faster and faster, and if they do not board it soon they will be left behind. But they are so used to jumping on moving trains, that they can afford time to throw a number of stones. Another thing in the tramp's favour is that they only have a few stones in the first place, and then have to pick them up. But what favours the tramp most is that these men cannot aim straight, because the train is on the move, and they have to follow the car. This was one of my worst experiences, being stoned while riding the rods. Of course these brakesmen could rush forward and either pull a tramp out or push him off, but they could not do so without getting him caught in the wheels. This would be such plain murder that, in spite of their rage, it frightens them; so they stone him instead, and give him a chance for his life. Half the tramps in America will not ride a train if they cannot get the comfort of an empty car—not even on a road where the brakesmen are good and indifferent as to the number of tramps they carry. Still, there are so many that have had my experience that I would not mention it in the hearing of an old American tramp.

But it must not be supposed that the dangers of beating one's way on freight trains in America are always caused by unsympathetic brakesmen. I know one good road which carried hundreds of tramps every week, and it was never known that a brakesman had ever put one off. In fact the brakesmen on this road used to look with indifference on tramps, as though they were part of the common freight. Some of these brakesmen were so used to tramps that they would confess a fear to run a train that had none, much the same as sailors look for rats on board a ship. But this road was spoilt by a gang of half robbers and half beggars. These men would board a train when it was standing still, and as soon as it was on the move, would go from car to car and search every man that they saw beating his way. This they would do with men riding outside, in coal cars or on flat cars. When the train stopped, they would get off and inspect the train. If they saw an empty car that contained one or two men, this gang—four, five, or six in number—would get in. A tramp would not know but what they were the same as himself, and would not feel any alarm, but welcome their company. But as soon as the train was again on the move, these new arrivals would then begin to question and search the first occupants of the car, and woe betide the man that refused to be searched or was not civil. Out through the open door he would be thrown, and the train would be going thirty or forty miles an hour, and it would be night. As I have said, these men were all beggars, for they would not make enough out of these petty robberies to keep them. For this reason a man had only to say, when questioned as to what he was, "I am a beggar," and they would then treat him with every respect. The men they wanted to find were those that were working men and had money in their pockets, but preferred to ride free on an easy road. The desperate methods of these men were so well known that tramps would often swarm together in one car, knowing that their number would make them safe. For all that, several dead men were found every week on this road, and the cause was well known to tramps. Some of the mutilated men that just escaped with their lives would have mentioned these things to the police, but the latter did not trouble, for it was all tramp work, from beginning to end.

One of the worst experiences I have ever heard of was of a young cattleman whom I knew in Baltimore. When I met him he was only a lad of twenty years, and he had such a calm, pleasant face that no one would think that he ever had an hour's suffering in his life. Two years before this he had been a stowaway from England to America, and he was not discovered for several days. So, being too late to put him on shore, the captain set him to work, with the intention of handing him over to the police on arrival in America. But when they were in sight of land and saw the distant lights, it being night, this lad possessed himself of a life-belt and, without being seen, dropped overboard. He was under the impression that the tide and his own exertions would take him to land before morning and, no one being about, he would be safe. But instead of this, he got caught in a strong outgoing current, and was taken out to sea. He then had the experience of floating two days and two nights in the deep sea, before he was seen and picked up by a passing ship. Whatever his thoughts could have been, it was most certain that his mind was not affected, for when I knew him he was the most cheerful and sweetest tempered in the cattleman's office, and he was never heard to mention his experience.

At this office was another cattleman, who had not only been in the hands of lynchers, but even had the rope round his neck and the other end of it thrown over the limb of a tree. A tramp had assaulted a woman, and a number of men were searching for him. Seeing a man at a camp-fire in the woods they at once pounced on him and, without any question, placed the rope round his neck and prepared to hang him. But, fortunately for him, another body of men came, led by the woman's husband, and with him was a little boy who had witnessed the assault. "That's not the man," said the little fellow—which saved the man's life. This cattleman was one of the ugliest men that I have ever seen, but he was really so harmless, simple, and innocent, that we all liked him and fed him, and got him to sing. We knew that women would be afraid of him, and for this reason he was apt to starve. So we better looking and less deserving tramps saved the poor fellow the humiliation of having doors slammed in his face, and hearing keys turned and bolts drawn.

Chapter IX

The American Lakes

English sailors who run away from their ships in America, often do so with the intention of going inland and sailing on the fresh-water lakes. Other sailors, who have done so before, but felt that they had to return to the salt sea, talk of their former experience, so that almost every English sailor knows what sailing on the American lakes is like. On their deep-sea boats they get hard biscuits, salt meat, dried peas, and cheap molasses; but on the lakes they get soft bread, fresh meat, green vegetables, and luxurious fruit. It is no lie that common sailors and firemen on the American lakes get strawberries and cream, when such berries are in season, and other fruits when they are not. Therefore it is not to be wondered at when English sailors soon feel themselves in a strange position: they feel loth to break away from the splendid board and lodging on fresh water, and yet cannot help feeling restless to return to the salt sea and take long voyages. There are hundreds of English sailors on the American lakes that have either been in our navy or merchant service, and they live so well, in comparison with their deep-sea experience, that it is a great pity that fresh water cannot employ them all the year, as the sea could. Of course, they earn enough to keep them idle during the winter, but we all know that saving sailors are almost as scarce as white crows.

The real fresh-water sailor, who has never been on the sea, and probably never saw it, is different to the deep-sea man in many ways. For instance, he walks straight and does not roll, which is owing to the different action of inland waters. His voice is gentle and soft, not rough and hoarse like a deep-sea sailor's. But, for all that, when it comes to money matters he is quite as extravagant as the man of long voyages, and is quite as easily fleeced by land-sharks, in spite of his greater knowledge of life on shore. And every lake town is as well supplied with land-sharks as a seaport of its size. But, fortunately for these lake sailors, they are nearly all beggars, owing to having no work in the winter when the lakes are frozen and navigation has stopped. This being the case, most of them think very little of begging a house, and if they are robbed or spend their money foolishly and have to wait for a ship, they are not likely to suffer hunger.

One great advantage on the lakes is that when a man ships he has no particular need of top boots, oilskins, and many other things needed by the man of the deep sea. Indeed, the latter has to even supply himself with a knife, fork, and spoon. There is no law that a man must have a bag of clothes, for there is no need of them. He is allowed to ship as he stands, no matter whether he is clad like a sailor or a farmer, or is in rags like an unsuccessful beggar. As far as appearances are concerned, a great number of these fresh-water sailors end the season as they began it. Some of them look far worse, for they may have had good clothes and boots when navigation began, and have worn them all the summer and have not bought others. Therefore, when they are paid for their last trip, and spend the money foolishly, they are ill-shod and shabbily dressed. The fresh-water sailors are not nearly so illiterate as salt-water men, because they are so often on shore in large towns and cities. A popular song would not be more than three or four days old before they were on shore to hear it. They do not return, after one voyage, to be surprised that the town has built a large new dock since they left, or doubled its population, as deep-sea men may do.

I was never, in all my life, seized with so great a desire for work as when I was in one of these lake towns and haunting the waterside. When I thought of the good pay, the rich food, and the easy work to be done, it was as much as I could do to keep from applying for a ship. In fact I made a special journey to Toronto for that very purpose, but was petted and spoilt by the many good people in that town. The first day I arrived I happened to find a green, open space where I could lie down and take my ease between meals. It did not take me long to find out that the houses around that green common were very good, for I had no difficulty at all in begging my first meal, which was breakfast. After doing this, I returned to the green common and lay down in the grass. But it was not long before the children came; so, wanting an active hour, I began to play ball with them. This exercise gave me a good appetite for dinner, and, when that hour came, I succeeded with as much ease as at breakfast-time. It was not long before I was back on the common, where I played ball with the children all the afternoon. Naturally, I now lost all inclination for work on the lakes, and even laughed at myself for ever having had such a thought. But, unfortunately, this life was too good to last long, for something happened the following day that not only put an end to my ball-playing, but forced me to leave the green common. I had gone to a house to seek dinner, and the door was answered by a man who, to my surprise, frowned at me. This unkind reception was so unusual on the great American continent that I made up my mind to demand, after he had refused me some dinner, an explanation as to why he received me in that way. But there was no need for me to speak, for the explanation came at once. "Look here," said he, "do you mean to tell me that you are looking for work?" "Nothing is more certain," I answered. "What!" he shouted; "didn't I see you playing ball with the children all day yesterday, only a few yards from here? Didn't I see you this morning holding the skipping-rope for some girls?" There was no escape from these questions, so I began to retreat. Perhaps that was the reason—that I had not made the least attempt to excuse myself—why he called me back and invited me indoors. And I must say that his good lady, who was smiling and laughing all the time, served me with an excellent dinner. In spite of this, I thought it wise not to be seen again in that happy green place, for fear that he might draw the attention of the police to me. So, being deprived of the pleasure of playing ball, I left Toronto, too down-hearted to seek enjoyment in any other part of that city, which was well known to be good all over.

I could nearly always be sure of a dollar or two at these lake towns—Chicago, Cleveland, Buffalo, Toronto, and others—owing to my acquaintance with so many men. For almost all the cattlemen that sailed from Baltimore in the winter, worked on the lakes in the summer. They left Baltimore a week or two before navigation began on the lakes, and as soon as it stopped they returned to work as cattlemen between America and Europe. As there were scores of these cattlemen, and I not only knew them all, but was liked, it was to my advantage to make lake towns my haunts. Not one of them ever insulted me with a hint that I should do as he did—work for my money. The reason of this is that they all considered it their duty to assist me, for I had often assisted them in other ways. For instance, when they came back one by one and in twos and threes from the lakes, they were always loth to start begging again in Baltimore, which they must either do or starve. To make things worse, they would probably have to wait a week or two before they could get a chance to sail with cattle, for at this time the office would be full of men. Now, as I was always back before them, they could rely on me for a little assistance, for I would beg extra on their account. But for all that, the money I got from them was more of a curse than a blessing, for the reason that it often kept me several days in idleness; and, after living in lazy respectability for three or four days, I always found it hard to start again to earn my living as a beggar.

It seems a mystery that these inland lakes should be sometimes visited by such terrific storms. One winter, when I was in Chicago, I went down to the waterside to see a ship in its last extremity. When I got there I saw thousands of helpless people, watching a vessel sinking before their eyes, no one being able to go to its assistance in small boats. We could expect to see this happen on the wild sea-coast, but this was an inland lake, and here was a city of more than a million inhabitants. It is more to be wondered at by men who have seen that beautiful lake almost without a ripple in summer-time.

Chapter X

The Happy Life

It is certainly a mystery how man got into this tangle, having to conform to the rules of civilization—up in the morning at a certain hour, and to bed at a certain time at night, with certain limited intervals for meals; in fact a very slave to these conditions, and so often without power of being otherwise. If he breaks his fetters by indulging in more sleep, or prolonging his meals, he will starve, for nuts are not now free for the picking, and fruits are not now the free gift of Nature; for she herself is made the servant of landlords who are tyrannical over their rights. It is only the small boys who occasionally defy such laws by robbing an orchard and putting to shame their big, cowardly fathers.

When I consider what pleasure it gives me to lie abed in the mornings at my own sweet will, I cannot help but feel pity for the great majority who must needs rise to answer the demands of civilization. Of course, I could not myself be so independent if I were not contented with very little, and did not prefer freedom to fine clothes and furniture and the luxuries of food.

We know very well that the one happy hour in the week for a man of business is when he wakes on a Sabbath morn, or a holiday, at his usual time to rise, and finds, O joy! that he is privileged to lie in bed, a free and a happy man.

What a strange contrast there is between the man who lives in a small house with just enough means, and no more, to keep him in idle content, and the man who, to keep up a position, has a large house with several servants, and worries himself night and day in business to keep things standing! What a wise man is the former, and what a poor fool is the latter! Position! What is it? It is to be pestered by invitations to other people's houses, and to be worried again in returning those invitations. How foolish is that business man, that he does not sell out and retire to a small country cottage, with his little income of a pound or twenty-five shillings a week, where he could eat, sleep, and read in peace, and walk abroad admiring Nature. Thousands of business men could do this, and would, if they were wise enough to see what an empty thing position is.

There are not many men in this world who appreciate more than I do that precious gift called sleep. When I wake in the morning and look at my watch, it may be seven o'clock. Then I question myself—"Shall I get up? If I do, what for? No, gentle Sleep, one more hour with thee." Then I sleep again and wake the second time, and ask this question again—"Shall I get up?" What with yawning and stretching it usually takes a quarter of an hour to answer, which makes the time quarter past eight. Then I say to myself, "I will count fifty before I get up." This I begin to do, very slowly; but when I have done I usually make the fifty a hundred. This dallying with time is very pleasant. Sometimes I return to bed after I have got up, and have even undressed for that purpose. To make a candid confession, I have—not often—got up, dressed, and then returned to bed with my clothes on, so as to enjoy another nap and be at no pains to dress again.

I remember making one trip on a cattle-boat, and on the return voyage to Baltimore there was no work to be done, we cattlemen being then counted as passengers. The nearest approach to work of any kind was that two men were commissioned each day to fetch food from the galley and to sweep the forecastle—the latter duty not to be strictly enforced. Now, it happened that there were fifteen cattlemen, so that one man would be exempt from even such petty duties as these. We therefore cast lots, and the laziest man was fortunate to win. It was Baldy, who, on hearing the decision, crept back into his bunk and remained there for the rest of the voyage. When the meals came, he sat up and requested some kind hand to pass him his food, and, after returning the empty dishes to the same kind hand, settled down for another sleep. One night the ship, being light, rolled so much that we were all thrown out of our bunks, all except Baldy. That same night we rushed on deck, cattlemen, sailors, and firemen, for the coal-bunkers had been broken in by the waves, and coal filled the galley, and the cattle-pens were smashed and taken to sea, and crash followed crash until we thought our end had come—and yet Baldy, whatever his feelings were, never left his bunk.

When we arrived at Baltimore we were all, as usual, without money. On Baldy being roused and told we were about to go ashore, he began slowly to rise, but it was only after making several attempts that he succeeded in standing on his feet. My heart went out in pity for the poor fellow, for it was as much as three of us could do to get him up the forecastle steps. It was with great difficulty that he passed the doctor, for that gentleman happened to see him totter, and he had an idea that Baldy and, in fact, all the crew should be quarantined; but on receiving an explanation that Baldy's legs were weak through inactivity, he allowed us to go ashore. The distance to the cattlemen's office was over a mile, and poor Baldy could not possibly walk that distance, and, as I have said, we were all without money. But as luck would have it, a gentleman saw Baldy's condition and gave him five cents to pay car fare, so we helped the poor fellow into the car, which would take him right to the door of the office.

Honestly, if I had not been cursed with ambition to excel in literature, I would have remained a beggar to the end of my days; to winter in such towns as Baltimore, and spend my summer months in travelling through the green country, with short stops here and there in cities and large towns.

What a life it is! To study faces and the strange humours of different people. Yes, when I was about to call at a house for my dinner, the Baltimore Kid suddenly clutched my shoulders, and said impressively: "Whatever you do, do not address that woman as Lady, but call her Madam, or Mrs." Just to humour the

Kid, for I thought such advice was ridiculous, I addressed the lady as Madam, and explained my needs. She motioned me to a small, wooden outhouse, which I entered, and seeing a chair and a table, sat down. In about two minutes the lady reappeared, carrying a hot dinner, for which I stood, as became a gentleman, and thanked her, saying: "I thank you, Madam," but was almost on the point of saying "lady." After having had dinner, I went to the back door and knocked, to thank her for her kindness. "You are quite welcome," she said; "the only people I refuse are those who say 'lady,' for I have cause to believe that such people are professional beggars." You see, by this instance, how one little word can assist or spoil a man in his profession.

The Baltimore Kid was one of the keenest beggars in America. The sight or sound of money put the very devil in him. If he heard coins rattling in the pockets of a passer-by, he would follow that person side by side, up one street and down another until he had succeeded in talking the man out of a coin. If he saw a lady open her purse, he was at once at her side, and explaining his position. He boasted that he had begged the President, when the latter was visiting his paternal home. The Kid had intended to beg the house for clothes, but, seeing the President alone in the garden, quickly altered his mind. He claimed to have then talked the gentleman out of a five-dollar bill. Whether this story was true or not, I cannot say, but I am certain of one thing—that it was only the want of opportunity that would keep it from being attempted. The pomp and splendour of Solomon's throne would not have daunted the Baltimore Kid, if he saw the way clear of stern guards and meddlesome attendants. Many of the great capitalists of America, and many Europeans of title, had succumbed to the Kid's voice. Yes, he has often related to me how easy he found the Grand Duke of Gorgonzola, and how long it took to convince Tomkins the millionaire butcher.

Chapter XI

Boy Desperadoes

The danger of our slums is not caused so much by men as by boys; and some of the latter are so young that they have not yet taken to drink, although they have smoked cigarettes for years. These half boys and half men are far more dangerous than full-grown bullies. The reason is that they do not think of the consequences, and they work themselves into an hysterical passion that often results in brutal murder. One time I was in a small town in America when a young outlaw of eighteen years was being tried for killing about half a dozen men, and half killing a number of others, all in his short career. No doubt this sounds like very high brutal courage, but the truth of the matter is that it was the lowest cowardice. He was too young to have that cool courage of a man who bids another to stand and deliver and, after committing robbery, walks away without more ado. This boy, full of fear, no sooner saw the motion of another than he pulled the trigger, in fear of his own life. I don't suppose that there was ever a man outlaw in America that was so dangerous as this youth. Again, men are robbers for gain, and nothing else; but when a number of these half boys and half men are together, they want sport and romance as well. They would not be satisfied with robbing a man, but would like to show their power after. What makes these youths so dangerous is that they obey the first impulse, which, more often than not, is a cruel one; and the cruelty increases with their strength of number.

One time I saw a dozen boys on the levee in St. Louis hold up and rob every man they came to. They not only did this, but, as usual with them, started to beat the man after, kicking and punching him, until he had to run for his life. This happened in broad daylight; but they took care, as hysterical as they were, not to interfere with more than two men at a time, in spite of their number. These boys were quite dangerous, with revolvers, razors, knives, and clubs; and they uttered the most fearful oaths, and yelled like savages. No doubt, if they had met a stubborn man, who refused to either escape or humour them, they would have killed him. Now, what could a man do against these blind, desperate young bullies? If he had a revolver, he could hold back a dozen men by threatening to shoot the first man that advanced, and each man would have had enough sense to see the folly of risking his life. But these youths would have rushed on in their blind passion, and whether you shot one or not, you could not escape being half killed or killed by the others. These half boys and half men have no idea of fair play; if a man goes down, they will take good care that he does not rise again to renew the battle, for they will kick him into unconsciousness.

It is these young bullies, and not grown men, that make the slums of London and other large cities so dangerous. They feel the strength of the coming man, and they are eager to try it. So, when they see a man drunk, and scarcely capable of looking after himself, they begin to jibe him. The poor fool, courageous in drink, and seeing that they are no more than boys, stops to abuse them. It is then that one of them steps forward and sometimes, to disguise his intention, holds out the hand of friendship, and the poor drunkard receives a blow in the face instead. Of course, this exasperates him, and he attacks them all. If it is day, the young bullies escape laughing, but if it is night, and the place quiet, they will all try their strength on him, and probably leave him insensible in the gutter. If they cannot trip a man or knock him down, they kick or use the buckles of belts, and they give him great cause to remember the occasion. Nearly all these young bullies wear strong leather belts with heavy solid buckles, and they know well how to use them.

Any common lodging-house that harbours a gang of five or six of these half boys and half men is a very dangerous place in which to live. If there is a full-grown bully there, he will be very cautious not to offend any of these, however he may try to intimidate other lodgers. I left one lodging-house, after staying there a week, because of three of these young ruffians, who seemed to do as they liked. At that house there was a big bully, a man six feet in height and heavy in build. This big fellow was continually grumbling and threatening the old lodgers, but never interfered with the younger ones, although they often laughed at him in mockery. But one day, when he was cooking at the fire, one of these young ruffians, accidentally it seemed, pushed him, and the big bully turned with his usual oath and uplifted hand. Now, no doubt, if the kitchen had been empty, he would have pretended to be satisfied with the young ruffian's sneering apology, but seeing so many witnesses, he thought it was his duty to show what he was, so he gave the youngster a slap in the face. The latter did not attempt to retaliate, for he had not the assistance of his friends. No doubt he told them of it that night, when they were all together. A few mornings after this the big bully was found dead in bed; his death being caused by a blow in the back of the head, received in a fall. It seemed that he had had enough strength to walk to the lodging-house and get into bed, and had died afterward. There were several beds in that room, but none of the other lodgers had heard anything unusual in the night, although they saw that the man staggered into the room. There can be no doubt but what he was drunk, but drunken men do not often fall down and deal themselves death-blows—they only collapse. My opinion is that these young ruffians had waylaid him away from the house, and seeing that he was drunk, helped him to his fall. These young bullies never forgive, and never forget. If one is threatened when he is without the support of others, he will not rest satisfied until he gets their help and takes vengeance.

What makes full-grown men so much afraid of these half boys and half men is their entire recklessness. They will use knife, poker, fork, or anything that is near their hands. One day I saw one of these young bullies deliberately poke an old man's eye out. The man was well known to be very quiet and not at all ill-tempered; and when he asked that the table should not be shaken because of his tea—this boy sprang to his feet and, without a word, poked the old man's eye out. A cruel, unfeeling action of this kind would never enter the mind of a full-grown man, however great a bully he might be; only an impulsive, irresponsible youth of this kind would do such a deed.

In some lodging-houses the manager will not let beds to more than two of these half boys and half men, for he knows from experience the trouble they make; and that old and quiet lodgers will fear them so much that they will go elsewhere. For these young bullies have no sympathy with age or affliction, and it would not be well for a blind man to expect them to use restraint and humour him in everything. They feel the strength of manhood coming on them, and they do not know what to do with it. All these lads are out of steady employment and doing a few odd jobs often too light for them, and their growing strength is not getting sufficient use. So, when they are standing at street corners, they are always eager for action, and the man that takes notice of their insults or missiles, will most likely soon be in a pitiful state. It is these sober young bullies that smoke cigarettes at street corners, and not full-grown bullies in public houses, that a stranger has to fear. The latter make enough noise, when they are going home at night, singing or fighting among themselves, but they seldom interfere with strangers. But the young bullies, that are neither boys nor men, allow their animal spirits full play, and are only too eager to interfere with anyone.

Chapter XII

American and English Beggars

A man that has camped out much in the open air must always after be on the look-out for places suitable for camps. So whenever I cross over a country bridge, under which runs a narrow stream, I often stand and look along the stream's banks in quest of a shady tree to sit out of the sun, happy to know that I can seek shelter under the bridge in case of rain. Yes, there is plenty of dry wood for cooking purposes, and fresh water in a delightful state of activity, and the bridge to be my shelter in a storm— such is an ideal spot for a camp. If I find this place in England there will be seen a sign that trespassers will be prosecuted, and for that reason the spot remains, and will remain, in its virgin state, untrodden by the foot of man. But if I am in America I shall not see that sign, and therefore at once take possession, and I know well that I shall find embers of past fires, and a quiet search in the adjoining bush will bring to light the rude cooking utensils used by former occupants.

Alas for the strict regulations that govern this overcrowded land of ours! If I have a houseboat I cannot move it without first apprising the river commissioners and having their consent to do so. If I use a bit of wild woodland, untilled, and without fruit, cattle, or any other money-making stock, I am ordered to put out my fire by a man who can produce papers to show his authority. Our liberties extend so far, and no farther, and we are not free to periodically enjoy the sweet open-air life of our ancestors. A free country indeed! Even if I own a cottage, with a piece of land, and have my title deeds to show for it, the sporting gentry can over-run it after a fox. And, although compensation can be claimed for damage done to a field of turnips, I would be laughed at for a mad eccentric if I asked compensation for the rude trampling of my garden flowers. But things are different in America, and, for that matter, in all new countries. The woods belong to all comers and all that is found therein—sunny glades and shady trees, birds, springs, flowers, and squirrels. No stranger to demand by what authority I camp there; and any respectable stranger that chanced to come near would no more think of entering my camp without an invitation than he would of entering my town house. For in America it is customary for all classes of families to forsake their homes for a few days in the summer and camp out, sometimes only on the outskirts of the town and within easy distance of their homes. These outings cost little, are healthy, and the whole family are together; and it only requires care that the smallest and youngest does not roll into the rill and get drowned—a rill that in certain parts is often as much as three inches deep.

But the man to whom this kind of life properly belongs is the American tramp. His camp is to be found on the outskirts of every town, either on the northern, southern, eastern, or western end; and it is not uncommon to find a camp at each end. The camp is his great institution, a club and private residence; from which he sallies on his begging expeditions, and to which he returns with his spoils; at which place he cooks, eats, reads, discourses, takes his afternoon nap, washes his clothes, or discards them for others lately acquired. There they build their fires near running water, around which they sit at night and relate their day's experience.

The Baltimore Kid was that morning offered work, but had taken the insult good-naturedly, having retired without wasting time in excuses. His companions laugh heartily at this, to imagine the Kid at work, and Philadelphia Baldy enquires philosophically, "What is work, boys?" These men are all downrighters; that is, none of them make any pretence of selling cheap goods, but beg food and money straight.

Begging in England is certainly a fine art, and it is very difficult to live except beggars carry in their hands pins, needles, laces, wire goods, artificial flowers, a tin whistle, accordion, etc., and hide themselves as beggars behind these things. Even then they make very little, if they are indifferent to the art of begging; for it is not sufficient to sell a farthing pair of laces for a penny, but to tell such a pitiful story that the buyer—out of pity for your misfortunes—returns the laces after paying for them, and occasionally adds a piece of cake to her kindness. That is the real art of begging; and the man who cannot make threepence or more out of a farthing stud, a farthing's worth of pins, or a farthing pair of laces, is no more than a very small and unsuccessful business man, and is not worthy the name of a beggar.

The art of begging is not nearly so fine in America as it is in England, for there is no necessity in that country of making any pretence of selling; and money, food, and clothes are to be had for the mere asking. The American beggar uses few words, for he knows well that whoever can afford will give, and he is too cunning to employ pitiful tales, which would be apt to encumber him with a quantity of common bread and butter, from people who have nothing ready cooked. For this reason he pockets the few trifles in the way of sandwiches and cakes, and proceeds leisurely from house to house, until he is seated at the table like a Christian, and supplied with a hot meal, which is the end he seeks, and which seldom fails. After which he returns to the camp, unloads his pockets of their trifles, and reads, and talks with his companions until supper-time, which we in England call tea-time. Then he takes a tin can to the spring, places it full of water on the fire, and makes hot coffee, with which he devours his trifles. He has had a hot breakfast and a hot dinner, and he is quite satisfied to eat one meal a day that only consists of cold meat, bread and butter, and a cake or two.

The American tramp sits comfortably at his camp fire, waiting the sound of a shrill whistle, or bell, which proclaims dinner-time. Five or ten minutes after hearing this sound, he dances out of camp, humming a tune, and goes begging as though he were going to a wedding, and he is often served with a hot dinner before the man of business can finish his own. But the poor English beggar makes funeral steps between meals, and asks for a mouthful of bread. The American beggar pulls the door bell, and makes himself heard the first time; but the English beggar timidly uses his knuckles on the back door, many times before he is heard. The American beggar rides on trains from town to town, but the English beggar tramps the hard roads. The English beggar explains his wants to the servants and children, but the American beggar asks to see the mistress. The American beggar, feeling himself a proud and free citizen, addresses himself familiarly to anyone; but the English beggar, feeling himself a despised outcast, will not speak except in want, or when he is first spoken to.

Yes, begging in America is fascinating, without doubt; and it is no wonder that the tribe has increased to such an enormous extent. But in England it is such a fine art, and requires so much persistence to attain small ends, that there are few that can master it thoroughly. What did Chicago Fatty do when he visited Liverpool on a cattle-boat? He asked forty men for a copper towards paying for a fourpenny bed, and the result was twopence threefarthings—and the workhouse. Begging in England nearly broke his heart and so sickened him that, when he returned to his own country, New York Slim and Boston Shorty had to feed him, as though he were a babe in arms, until he recovered sufficiently to help himself. Blacky— the half-breed—who claimed to have enough Indian blood in his veins to make himself dangerous if he had cause—Blacky, I say, thought that Fatty would never again be a good beggar. It certainly seemed, for a long time, that this would be the case, until one morning Fatty went out and begged his breakfast, but nothing more. He went out again, begged a meal, a shirt, and a handkerchief. In a day or two this good beggar—almost ruined by a trip to England—began to take a man with him to carry the spoils, as he had been accustomed to do in his prosperous days.

Chapter XIII

Beggars' Slang

Women, strange to say, take far more pride than men in using slang. To listen to two women relating their experiences in a country common lodging-house is almost to hear a foreign language. I cannot think that a woman takes more pleasure or near so much, in a wandering, homeless life, as a man. Nevertheless, it is plain that women affect to enjoy it more. In fact, I have often heard women boast of being on the road a certain number of years, but have seldom heard a man take the trouble to mention such a thing. In spite of this, one thing proves that a woman of this kind speaks false and is trying to make the best of a strange life. It is this—when she and her husband are settled in a lodging-house, he is always the first to propose taking to the road again, and the woman always inclines to postpone that event for another day. If they are old travellers, they are sure to see in every lodging-house others they have met before, and that is why the woman would like to settle for a few days; but the man, being less sociable, is more restless. What surprised me, when I first went on the road in England, was to see how sociable these people were, calling each other by some kind of name, as though they had lived there always, or had always travelled together. It was some time before I discovered the reason of this. Naturally, my first impression had been that a score or more men and women would meet, coming from different towns, and not know each other; and, after having a night's lodging, would continue their travels and perhaps never meet again. But, to my surprise, I often entered a lodging-house where there would be a dozen lodgers or more, and I would be the only stranger there. I soon got to know that these temporary lodgers had been beggars for years, and one of them could not possibly appear in a lodging-house without meeting others he had met before. The reason of this is that most beggars have their favourite counties, which they seldom leave, and if they do not meet in a lodging-house they meet on the road. There are hundreds of beggars that work in a circle around London, within ten, fifteen, twenty, or thirty miles; and, seeing that some of them have been doing this for years, it is not surprising that they recognize one another at the different lodging-houses. The second night that I was on the road in England, I went to a lodging-house in Luton and, of course, expected to find a dozen or more strangers to the town, like myself, who would sleep there one night, part the next morning, and never meet again. But when I entered the kitchen I found a number of lodgers, men and women, who were calling each other by name—Brum, Norfolk, Sal, and Liz. In fact, I was the only stranger present, and yet all these were wanderers, and never travelled together. Very few of these were downright beggars, but had some trifle to sell. Their pride was in being able to beg under the disguise of selling.

I never knew that beggars had so many slang words until I had been on the road for several weeks and was in Gloucestershire. I had heard a number of strange words, but had not heard any sustained conversation. But one day, when walking from Stroud into Gloucester, I happened to meet a real beggar. It was close on evening and, as I had done well enough to be able to pay for my bed, I was making all speed to a lodging-house. Soon I heard quick steps behind me, and was overtaken by another beggar, who walked at my side and entered into conversation. Hearing where I was going to he asked me if I knew Gloucester and, if so, what lodging-house I intended to go to. Telling him that I did not know that town, and would have to enquire about a lodging-house, he at once offered to conduct me to one, saying that there were several and that he knew the best. I was very glad of this offer, and we trudged along in pleasant conversation. Now, this man's conversation was as pure from slang as mine, which surprised me, for he was an old beggar, though perhaps not over thirty-five years of age. I may as well say here what kind of begging the man was doing at this time of his life, which became known to me after, for I had his company for several days. He had taken advantage of the South African War, saying that he had been invalided home. As you may guess, he was a fraud, and had never been in the Army. This man carried forged letters, supposed to be recommendations from officers under whom he had served. With these he called at the houses of old, retired military men and others, sending the papers in by a servant. All he had to do was to find out the names and addresses of these old officers, one or two of whom are to be found near every little hamlet or village. This was not difficult, for he knew the counties of Gloucestershire and Monmouthshire well; and every lodging-house has a town beggar who can give names, addresses, histories, and describe the position and appearance of houses wanted. Very well, then, this beggar would go to the house of one of these rich, retired military officers and, when the servant opened the door, would give her his papers to be taken to her master. In a few moments she would return with the papers and probably a shilling or a two-shilling piece on top of them. As can be expected, this man had several times been so closely questioned that he had compromised himself, and had been threatened with prison as a fraud. However, he was so bold, and knew his subject so well, that this had not often happened. At the houses of rich civilians he was safer, but, naturally, they would not give so much as a gentleman who had served in the Army. At this stage of his career this ambitious beggar did not often call at small houses for pennies, but large houses for silver. I soon found out his history, for he seemed nothing loth to talk of himself. He had taken to the road early, not having worked for a living since he was a youth. In those early days he had worked for a printer, and had caught his little finger in one of the machines. This accident did not handicap him in any way, and was no excuse for his leaving at once and becoming a beggar. In after years he never forgot to call two or three times a year on the printer, who had a fine business, and hold up his little finger; an action which won him a piece of silver every time. It was by his little finger that he proved his identity— that he was the boy that had worked for the printer in years gone.

It was when I heard this man and another in conversation that I first became surprised at the number of slang words that beggars use. As I have said, he used no slang during our walk, but we had no sooner entered a lodging-house and he met a beggar he knew, than his language was completely changed. When we were entering the city of Gloucester, he had called at a big, red house, which he told me was always good for twopence and a parcel of food, no more or less. He explained to me that he would not go out of his way for it, but thought he may as well have it, seeing that he was passing the house. It was in relation to this house that he spoke to his companion, using the following words: "I called at the big, red kennel and got my eight farthings and scrand." To which the other said: "That kennel never yet failed a needy." This conversation quite interested me; kennel was house; eight farthings was twopence; scrand was food; and needy was beggar.

Beggars in London lodging-houses use the slang of lodging-houses, and not of the road. They always say "fourpence for 'doss' or 'kip'"; but true, wandering beggars say "sixteen farthings for the feather." The former say "chuck" or "tommy," when they refer to food; but the latter say "scrand." The wandering beggar says "skimish" for drink, but city beggars say "bouse." The word "mouch" is not often heard outside towns, for wandering beggars say "call." For instance, "it is a good road to call," or "there is plenty of calling"; meaning that the road has many houses. They often use the word "lay." When a beggar asks another if a certain town is good, the former is asked, "What is your lay?" or, "It depends on your lay"; meaning: "What do you do—sell, sing, or go in for downright begging?" What always surprised me was to hear old beggars use the dignified word "travellers," in preference to beggars, needies, or callers. When they are talking of a good town, they say "it is good for travellers." And if they see a selfish lodger monopolizing the fire, or not making room on the table for others, they say "he's not a true traveller."

The following are a few slang words used by beggars:—

Beggars—travellers or needies; house—kennel; on the road—on the toe be; talk—patter; sing—griddle or chant; fourpence—sixteen farthings; bed—feather; soup—shackles; profit—bunts; food—scrand; drink—skimish; pins—pricks; needles—sharps; laces—stretchers; scissors—snips; combs—rakes; spectacles—glims; pictures—smuts.

XIV

Bony's Wits

We called him "Bony," because he was all skin and bones. This condition must have been constitutional, for it certainly was not from too much activity, seeing that he went by tram on his expeditions, and returned in the same manner. Again, it could not have been for want of good food, for Bony was a good beggar, and scorned to sit down to a bread-and-butter meal. He was also a good ale drinker, and, if his bones had been capable of growing flesh, it is very likely that ale would have helped to bring about that result. He was always heard to be humming a tune—often an old familiar hymn—so that it could not have been mental worry that fastened his skin so tight to his bones. No, his condition must have been constitutional.

I had known Bony for several months, and now that I had fallen on evil times, and would in less than a week be compelled to travel the country, I thought that perhaps my friend Bony could give me a few hints, that would assist me in procuring food and lodgings. Therefore, one evening, after he had had tea and was emptying his pockets of tram fare tickets, I invited him outside to have a drink. This invitation he would accept only on one condition—that I would then have another with him. Having no objection to this, we left the house together, and were soon comfortably seated in the warm corner of an alehouse.

After we had had the second drink, I began by asking Bony what he considered to be the most essential gift for a good beggar. Without immediately answering this question, he called for two more drinks, and, after they had been served, and he had praised the colour of the ale, he began. "The one thing, above all others, is to have ready wit, so as to take advantage of opportunities that come and go in a second, and give no time for second thoughts. For instance," continued Bony, "when I was in the country some time ago, I called at a house for a glass of water. I did not think that there was the least prospect of getting tea, as the time was between meals; therefore, being dry, I asked for water. A little girl answered the door, and after hearing my wants, returned to tell her mother. 'Certainly,' said the mother; 'he could have had a cup of tea, if he had asked for it, but perhaps he prefers water.' These words were said so low that they could not have been heard, except by a man who had all his wits about him. So, when the little girl returned with the water, I told her, in a voice loud enough to be heard in the house, that I was really sick for a hot drink of tea, but that it was not the tea-hour, and I must be content with water. I lifted the glass of water slowly to my lips, so slowly that the lady had heard my remark, weighed it for a second, and then promised a cup of tea, before my lips had touched the water. And, of course, the kind lady asked me if I would like a piece of cake to eat with the tea. You see," continued Bony, "how a man needs to keep his wits at work. Nine beggars out of ten would not have heard or, having heard, would have accepted the water and cursed themselves inwardly that they had not asked for tea." I was so interested in this recital that I called for two more drinks.

"Again," said Bony, after praising the colour of the liquor, "I happened one day to see a lady and gentleman approaching, and determined to accost them. As they drew near, I saw a crust of bread on the road, and that was my chance. Casting a hasty look behind me, as though I did not wish to be seen, I stooped, picked up the crust, and pretended to take a bite; and then I feigned seeing them for the first time, and hastily concealed the crust in my clothes. That little trick worked out well, for the lady gave me sixpence, and the gentleman gave me a shilling, and not a word passed between us."

Bony now called for two more drinks, and, after remarking that the colour of the ale was getting no worse, continued his experiences.

"One day," he began, "I was walking the high-road when a gentleman on a bicycle ran into me, knocking me down and throwing himself into the hedge. It did me no harm at all, for I was soon on my feet and going to his assistance. All my consideration was for him, thinking he might be seriously hurt. To my surprise he was not, but much shaken. After he had sufficiently recovered his breath he looked towards me and said: 'Are you hurt, my poor man?' Quick as a flash it occurred to me that I was, and I began to limp painfully. 'How far are you going?' he asked. I mentioned a town four miles away, and said that I had no doubt but what I could walk there, but that on my reaching that place it would probably be a week or more before I would be able to work, even if I could get it, and that I had no means whatever to keep myself idle in lodgings for that length of time. 'Are you sure that you can walk there without assistance?' he asked. 'Yes,' I said, 'by taking my time.' 'I am very sorry for you,' said he, 'and if this can be of help you are heartily welcome to it'—with that he placed in my hand a gold half-sovereign. Telling him I was ashamed to take advantage of what was no more than a pure accident, but that my straitened circumstances compelled me to do so, and saying how glad I was that he received no hurt, I left him, and began to limp painfully on my way. I had not got many yards, when he was again at my side, and, giving me his card, asked me to write in the course of a day or two, and let him know of my progress. And, you may depend on it," said Bony, with a grin, "that I did write on the third day, saying that I was doing well—for I feared a personal visit from him, with a doctor—and that in three or four more days I would be in a fit condition to work. He wrote a very kind letter in answer, with a postal order enclosed for ten shillings. Of course, I still keep the gentleman's address, and call on him occasionally, and I always receive a good meal and a shilling, and sometimes clothes as well."

"Have another drink, Bony," said I.

After the drinks were brought, and Bony had passed his usual comment on the colour, he went on to tell how necessary it was to keep a civil tongue on all occasions. "One day," said he, "a little man whom I could have crushed in my arms, called me all the big, idle vagabonds he could think of. But I allowed him free speech, knowing that he would be so pleased to see a man timid, who was almost twice his size, that he would at last become generous out of sheer delight, and such was the case.

"On another occasion I called at a lady's house, and received sixpence for my trouble, which was the first bit of silver that I had seen for several days, and for which I thanked her from the bottom of my heart. She stood at the door, as I was leaving, and said: 'Poor, unfortunate man!' 'Madam,' I answered, returning, for I was almost at the gate—'Madam,' I said, 'I am thankful to say that I am not half so unfortunate as my poor brother, who has weak intellect.' 'Oh, I am deeply moved to hear that,' said the kind lady, 'and will give you another sixpence for your poor brother.'

"These incidents," continued Bony, "prove how necessary it is to have quick wits. Only last week, within a mile of this alehouse, I got a two-shilling piece from a man in a very simple manner. I had been calling at the alehouses all the evening, and was returning home with three or four shillings worth of coppers in my pockets, not to mention the pleasant effect on my system of several free drinks of good strong ale.

"When I was on the bridge, I had my attention drawn to the sound of voices in a small boat running under the bridge, which made me pause and, leaning on the balustrade, look down into the river. This was not done so much from curiosity, but that I was beginning to feel tired. At that hour of the night the bridge was almost deserted, and I was just on the point of moving on when a gentle hand fell on my shoulder, and a voice kind and earnest said: 'Don't, I entreat you, destroy your immortal soul; don't, my dear brother, plunge into the dark waters.' I must confess that, for one moment, my wits entirely deserted me, and if the speaker had not still held me in his grasp, and continued his persuasion, I should have been foolish enough to explain that such was not my intention. But I soon recovered from my astonishment, and allowed him to lead me over the bridge. When we stood safely on the other side, he asked me what could be done to save me from self-destruction. Of course I had by this time recovered my wits, and told him a harrowing tale of misfortune, which earned me that gentleman's pity to the extent of two shillings. After receiving my promise that I would live and face misfortune like a man, he left me, and I, well pleased at such good fortune, sought my lodgings."

These incidents, as related by Bony, proved to me how necessary it was for a man to be quick-witted, if he would excel as a beggar.

After several more drinks we left for home, for the colour of the ale did not seem so good as when we first entered the place.

Chapter XV

Favouritism

One of the worst enemies to a poor man in a common lodging-house is favouritism. I have seen hundreds of instances where a man could be comparatively happy were it not for a prejudiced porter or kitchen-man. I was not long in one large house before I saw this, in the case of a porter, a bully, and a gentleman. The bully was drunk and going from place to place, insulting everyone, especially those that were better dressed than himself. Few of the lodgers took any notice of him, until he came to one that had on a silk hat and a frock-coat. This man lost his temper and told the bully that he had no right to interfere with men that wanted to be quiet. He was in the act of uttering this dignified rebuke when a porter came and stood before them. "What's the matter?" he asked. The well-dressed man began a quiet explanation, but the bully interrupted him; so the former stopped at once, thinking he would have a chance to speak when the other had done. "You had better go to bed," said the porter to the bully, "and"—addressing the well-dressed man—"you come with me to the office." When they arrived at the office the porter said a few words to the clerk, and the latter returned the well-dressed man his money, telling him to go elsewhere for a bed. There were very few lodgers in the house that did not know the meaning of this injustice. The well-dressed man was a gentleman, and, in spite of his low circumstances, did not forget it. He looked on the porters as his servants and, when he met them in the street, never invited them to have a drink. Again, there was no necessity for him to rise early, whereas the bully gave a porter sixpence a week to be called every morning.

I was not many weeks at this house before I thoroughly understood these matters. One night, when I was going to bed, a man, who was quite tipsy, wanted to detain me in conversation, and I was doing my best to escape, when up the stairs ran one of the porters. "Why don't you go to bed?" he said to me. "You haven't to get up in the morning, and others have." This porter had not heard my voice, and he could see that the other man was drunk, but of course he set upon me because the other paid to be called early. This porter became more civil after, which I could well understand. I used to tip the bath-porter twice a week, and seeing that they shared their tips—one being in a better position than another to get them—so, no doubt, the bath-porter had pointed me out for civility. There was no appeal against these porters. They allowed some men to do things which they got others turned out for, and it was no use trying to explain oneself to the manager. Although I believe that he was a very just man, he could not do otherwise than trust his men, say what they would. In fact, I believe that this manager was so just that he would have dismissed a porter at once if he could prove that that porter was prejudiced against any of the lodgers and having them turned out for his own spite.

When I left this house and went to one that was in the hands of Christianity, I found the same state of things. The Christian officer behind the food-bar gave thick slices of bread to those he liked and thin slices to others; and he skimmed the top of the soup for those he did not like or was indifferent to, but his ladle went to the bottom for favourites. The consequence was that some lodgers would have hot, greasy water, while others would have thick soup that was almost Irish stew. It was well worth while to bribe this man with a drink of whisky. One artful lodger did better than that, as he told me in confidence. This man behind the bar was not supposed to take money for food; the lodgers had to buy tin checks at the office, with which they paid for what they wanted. But my artful dodger would go to the bar when no one was there to see, put a penny down and receive what he asked for. The officer behind the bar would quickly take this money, in spite of the strict rules and the severe discipline of that Christian army. But if a newly-arrived stranger put money down, that officer would shout, loud enough to be heard at the office—"We don't take money behind the bar; go to the office for checks."

When I first went to that lodging-house I had a small bundle, in which were an extra shirt, a pair of stockings, a brush, razor, and a few other articles. Seeing that all the lockers were in use, I had no other option than to ask the kitchen-man to look after it, for which I gave him twopence, although he had no claim to anything. Whether the bar-man saw this deed or was told about it I cannot say, but I know that I soon became one of his favourites. I may as well say here that, judging by my later experience at this place, it was well that I did tip the kitchen-man, for he often took a notion to sell the things in his charge, only holding such property sacred as had been tipped for. And yet on a Sunday afternoon these two, the bar-man and the kitchen-man, would be seen one on each side of the captain, and heard crowing like two cocks that challenge each other. When the captain prayed one would shout "Hallelujah!" The other would no sooner hear this than he would stretch his neck, grow red in the face, and cry fiercely, "Praise the Lord!" These doings not only amused the lodgers, but the principals as well; for, judging by their faces, it was all they could do to keep from laughing outright.

I was at one lodging-house where the beds were clean, the cooking accommodation good, and, according to the small rent to be paid, everything as could be desired. But this place was also spoilt by a common kitchen-man, who made things uncomfortable for all those that did not give him either money, ale, or tobacco. This man would build the fire up when a disfavoured lodger was in the middle of cooking a meal, and then sweep the dusty floor when he was at his meals. Of course, these things had to be done, so that there was no use in reporting him to the manager. Still, there was no reason why he should make more dust around your food, and take longer under your table than others, and build up the fire before there was actual need of it. Yes, there was a reason—known to himself—you never gave him anything.

This kitchen-man upset me so much that I agreed with another lodger to share a furnished bed sitting-room. Alas! I was soon back in the same lodging-house, in spite of its crazy kitchen-man. The man with whom I shared the room disappeared suddenly, and when I heard his character I did likewise. Without my knowledge, he borrowed of the landlady; and the vicar came to me saying that my friend had told him that I was on the point of starvation, and got a shilling on that account. Not knowing what else he had done in the neighbourhood, I could not feel at ease. Therefore, not having the courage to give my landlady notice, I put on all my clothes—two pairs of trousers, two shirts, a waistcoat, two jackets, and an overcoat—and crept to the front door. Seeing that I had filled the pockets with a number of small articles, it did not surprise me much to find great difficulty in moving. I do not know what I would have done if the landlady had been at the front door, because I could not have squeezed past her, and she could not have helped seeing that I was as broad as I was long. What upset me was that she had said she would not have let the room to him, but had trusted my face. However, I did not owe her any rent, and if I ever meet her when I am better off I will give her a sovereign.

I have seen this favouritism even in prison. It came under my notice in an American jail, where I had to serve fifteen days, and I was as innocent as a new-born babe. All the prisoners were in one long room, with cells on each side, in which they slept at night. At the end of the room there was a square hole in the wall, which had a slide; and it was through this hole that the prisoners received their meals. When I went for my first meal, I could see the face of the old cook—who was a prisoner—and was rather surprised to see him nod and smile, as though he knew me. This smile was followed by a large plate of food, much more than others. Perhaps the old prisoner-cook thought he saw in me a fellow-prisoner in some other jail, and he may have been right, for I had been in many others; or perhaps I resembled a son of his. Whatever it was, it was quite clear that he did not give me the plate that came to my turn, but kept one apart.

Chapter XVI

A Law to Suppress Vagrancy

We are all deeply interested in any scheme that proposes to suppress the workhouse tramp, who has not only become a pest to the ratepayers of our country—who support so many workhouses—but has also brought the true beggar to his wits' end to earn a livelihood. To all true beggars, who systematically pursue their calling, the workhouse tramp has become as much of an eyesore as he is to the working classes of our land. This vagrant—whom the Law seems so much to disfavour—is, without doubt, a madman; but, if rightly dealt with, is not, I believe, incapable of being cured. That he will not work to maintain himself in a good home, with food, bed, and clothing; and that he prefers to break so many hundredweight of stone—a heavy task to be performed on a bowl of thin gruel, or limited supply of bread and water—that he prefers to do the latter is sufficient proof of the man's mental deficiencies. To turn such a one into a useful member of society would be to confer as great a benefit on him as on the ratepayer of this country. Sometimes he cavils at the injustice of such tasks, and is sent to prison for refusing to perform them; or, the task being done, he tears in shreds his old rags, thinking to obtain a new outfit at the ratepayers' expense. For this he is also sentenced; for, though he has without doubt earned a cheap suit of clothes, he is by no means entitled to any—not even to a pair of stockings. Of course, our workhouses are not hotels, neither are they rough boarding camps, so that the ratepayers are, after supporting them, far from being relieved, seeing that this tramp is forced to make personal application for more food, or starve. But what I mention is that this man works hard and gets little for his trouble, and that he could be made a useful member of society and obtain more necessities—aye, even luxuries—by performing far less labour.

For my own class, whom I as a proud member represent, the outlook is indeed serious. Only yesterday an incident occurred which will, I believe, explain how the workhouse tramp stands in the light of a true beggar. I had seen a gentleman approaching in the distance, and had in my own mind resolved that he should not pass without first hearing my story. Being a clean man, keeping myself well shaved and brushed, I had very little fear of disgusting him by my personal appearance, making him seek to escape my importunities. It happened as I expected. During my narrative he stood smiling for a minute or two, for, you may depend, I gave him no time for excuse or question. At last I finished, and stood waiting the result of my confessions, which had been unusually pathetic. "My good fellow," said he, "I have just given the last threepence to another unfortunate man, who apparently was in greater need of assistance; I am very sorry." There was no other course than to continue my journey, for it was impossible to talk money out of an empty pocket. In five minutes after I was hailed by a voice from the hedgerow, and, looking in that direction, saw the most ragged man I had ever set eyes on, with his matted hair a foot long. "Did you meet a gentleman on your way?" he asked. "I did," said I; "and what of that?" "That man," said this ragged tramp, "was a thoroughbred. He saw me sitting here and, without a word from either of us, he emptied his pocket into my hand"—saying which he withdrew his fingers from the palm of his hand and disclosed to my view three pennies. Now, here was a workhouse tramp—for he was no other, or he would at once have stepped into the road and accosted the gentleman—receiving unsolicited alms; and I, who earned my living by the use of my tongue, must suffer in consequence.

But the worst charge to be made against this class of vagrant is that he does, by reason of his workhouse experience, look on common bread as a luxury, and receives it with so many thanks, from the various people on whom he calls, that these people soon become impressed with the notion that dry bread can be applied with satisfaction as a poultice in every case. In this way he spoils the road for good beggars who, not going into workhouses, need coppers for their beds, and who always make use of that indefinite term "something to eat," but would not, on any account, remind their hearers of "a crust of dry bread."

Again, he spoils true beggars by his lack of system. A workhouse tramp has not that energy and concentration which is required for success. Sometimes he knocks at the first door in a street, after which he walks to the next street, where he knocks at the middle house, or perhaps the last; and, when the true beggar comes after him, and beholds this timid fool running from side to side of a street, he knows very well that the street is being spoiled, for he cannot tell exactly where the other has been. In a case of this kind it is best for the true, systematic beggar to go at once into the next street, and it is not unlikely then but what he will soon recognize the workhouse tramp at its other end. If the true beggar had no other system than this—running here and there to chance houses, at the sign of a green gate, or a church announcement in a front window—he would soon be so confused as to where he had, or had not been, that a good-sized town would in a very short time become useless to him.

To a true beggar the workhouse tramp is a mystery. The former cannot understand how the latter can perform such stone-breaking feats on a bread-and-water diet, and he wonders where lies the fascination of such a life. He, himself, though he may rise penniless in the morning, has confidence in the day's fulfilment, and he sometimes meets with a surprise in the shape of a piece of silver. Sometimes he calls at an alehouse, where a merry party is in full song, and to them he offers to render harmony, provided they will favour him with a collection. This proposition is invariably favoured, and the true beggar then flatters the loudest and most persistent singer of the party by giving him his cap to make that collection. Of course, he is offered a glass of ale before he begins, and during the intervals between verses he is not forgotten. As a rule he is not a sweet singer, but his voice is thought to be remarkable, especially if he sings a familiar air with a good chorus. If his hearers are half blind with drink, and incapable of using their feet, it is well for the true beggar to end his song with a dance. The most awkward shuffling will appear to them as the movements of lightning. This kindness on his part calls forth extra coppers and a more liberal supply of ale. Now, what happens to shame this true beggar, and to spoil him in the act of earning a livelihood? Why, one of these ragged workhouse tramps walks in and begs a drink of water. Water! mark you, when this true beggar is earning ale and money! Then what wonder that such a man should become an eyesore to all classes of men? He has no self-respect, for, whereas he often passes stores and houses without calling at them, he is nothing backward in making known his wants to true beggars. For sometimes he by accident picks up sixpence, works for it, or receives it unsolicited, with which he pays for his bed at a lodging-house. Then he, without shame or self-respect, begs tea of one, sugar of another, and makes himself a pest to all those who with an independent spirit do their begging outside instead of inside a lodging-house, as he does. It is fortunate for us that he does not get these sixpences often, and that he is compelled almost night after night to the workhouse for accommodation.

The question is not altogether without humour, for these workhouse tramps actually call themselves our brothers on the road. They stop us familiarly on our way, and ask for information of workhouses, as though we were one of themselves. One advises me not to go to a certain workhouse, for they will make me break stones all the day following, on a little dry bread and water. As though I ever, for one moment, dreamed that such a lot would be mine! "My good fellow," says I, "lodging-houses are made for true beggars, and not workhouses."

For the above reasons I have become deeply interested in any scheme to improve the condition of the workhouse tramp, for, as I have said, he is not only a burden on the ratepayers of the country, but mars the success of all true beggars. We are often, when in the act of begging money for our beds, told to go to the workhouse; which is owing to this workhouse tramp having communicated the intelligence that he would be satisfied with bread, and that he is not in need of money for a place to sleep, seeing that the workhouse can accommodate him. For he becomes hardened to the indignities and heavy tasks set before him, and at last looks on such a cold, wretched place as a home, aye, even as a playground.

Chapter XVII

Stubborn Invalids

It is a pathetic sight to see men dying in a lodging-house, fighting against death day after day. The few healthy men that are present are quite indifferent to life, and do not care if their health is impaired through breathing in the same room as a dozen consumptives. These healthy men are so thoughtless of themselves that they offer their dying comrades saucers of tea, after which they drink with their own lips perhaps on the same place as their unfortunate fellows used. I have offered many a one of these poor fellows a drink of tea, but was always very careful not to use the saucer after them. When they wanted to return my kindness, and I did not like to wound their feelings by refusing them, I always took a clean saucer from the shelf, instead of using theirs.

I well remember one man, who was in a terrible condition for the last three months before he was carried to the hospital. He was a man of about middle age, and his face was very white, and all day long he was coughing and spitting in the kitchen, with only enough strength in his body to take him to bed. Although I sat with my back to him at meals, I could not help but hear the poor fellow, and could not help a feeling of revulsion. In fact I began at last to look upon these consumptives as murderers who, by their stubbornness in not going to the hospital, were killing me and others with their breath.

Some of these men are in receipt of small pensions, or get a little assistance from relatives on the outside, and for this reason they die sooner; for they have more leisure than others—who must go out to earn a few pennies—at the coke fire. Little Punch is dead, who might have lived for many more years, had he not been kept indoors so much by outside assistance. In the spring this little fellow used to set off with his pack as a pedlar through the country, and when he returned at the end of summer was always in good condition, but was as bad as ever after a month in the lodging-house. I believe he could have prolonged his life ten or fifteen years, if he had rambled both winter and summer.

These men fight against going to the hospital and sit dying day after day, making no complaint; until the lodging-house keeper is surprised some morning to find them lying in bed, without the strength to rise. Even then they swear it is only temporary indisposition, and that after a few hours' rest they will be well again. Then the doctor is called, and then comes the ambulance; but it is too late, for if the men do not die on the way, they die soon after they reach the hospital.

Poor old Peter saw himself wasting away. He was six feet two inches in height, but thin enough to be exhibited. He kept himself alive by a merry heart, but his hollow, spasmodic laughter refused to make his body fat. Up to the last he affected great cheerfulness, but he could not cheat death any longer. It was impossible to feel any revulsion against Peter; he did not spit about the place, and though he was always coughing, the poor fellow had no strength to make a disturbing noise: he could not be heard if you were not seated next him. You could feel him cough, by the vibration of the bench or table, more often than you could hear him. I also believe that he had consideration for others, knowing that a sick man can make himself unpleasant. Peter did nothing but win pity and goodwill, and he returned it by endeavouring to be witty and cheerful.

Old Scotty Bill, the flycatcher, is also dead. Consumption did not claim him as a victim, for he died at the advanced age of eighty-three, which was wonderful for a man who had spent the best part of his life in a lodging-house. No doubt if he had lived under better conditions, he would have reached a hundred years with ease. All his interest was in flies. While other lodgers were discussing the abundance of fish in Billingsgate, Scotty could be seen counting the flies in the kitchen, as a sign whether he should go out with his fly-papers or not. His language was very bad, and the last words he was heard to utter surprised even those who were accustomed to him, by their unusual weight and speed. He was another stubborn invalid, and fought hard against going to the hospital. His death was quite characteristic, and I can hardly imagine it otherwise. He, like many another one, was found one morning helpless in bed, and the manager, seeing that he was very ill, in spite of his assurance to the contrary, sent at once for the doctor. But when the latter arrived he and the manager were surprised to find the bed empty. On making enquiries they were told that Scotty was in the kitchen, and it was there that they found the old man, reading a newspaper. In spite of this the doctor saw that Scotty was not in good condition and tried to persuade him to go to bed, but this the old man swore that he would not do, and demanded some reason for such a request. Then there was a whispered consultation between the manager and the doctor, and it was decided to send for the ambulance and have him taken to the hospital whether he would or no. Now Scotty had lived in that same lodging-house for over thirty years, and for that reason was well known in the locality. Therefore, when the ambulance arrived at the door, and a woman outside enquired of a lodger as to who the ambulance was for, and was told of Scotty Bill, the news soon spread abroad. In less than five minutes between twenty and thirty women had assembled at the door. These women of the slums were never very clean, and at the present time not one of them was in a fit condition to answer her own door; but they forgot this in their anxiety to see poor Scotty Bill and wish him a speedy recovery. At last the old man appeared, and it staggered him to see the number of women at the door. But when he heard them say, "Poor Bill"; and "Good luck to you, Scotty"; his fury knew no bounds. Standing with one foot on the step, he paused, and then poured forth such a torrent of abuse that some of the women lost all sympathy with him and feebly retaliated. He told them to go home and scrub their dirty faces, instead of coming there to watch him—and other things not fit to mention. It was, they confessed, the worst language they had ever heard—and more than one of them was capable of using very strong words. That was the last seen of Scotty Bill, and that was his dying speech, for he died on his arrival at the hospital.

I have heard of the death of a number more, men that lingered with such determination that it almost seems as if they have taken advantage of my absence and died; for they all seem to have gone one after the other since I left. "One-eyed" Jim is dead. A terrible cough he had, but his face and neck were always like raw beef. That one eye of his blazed with such power that I have often imagined the devil hard at work shovelling half a ton a coal a minute to supply its fierce light. He also went off suddenly, walking the kitchen floor on Monday, and lying cold and dead on the following day.

"Rags" is also dead, the great drinker; the man who when abroad complained that whiskey made him totter, whereas it was an earthquake, that tumbled towers and made the firm-footed houses reel. "The whiskey's in my legs," said "Rags," not knowing it was an earthquake.

"Monkey" Sam and the "Dodger" are both dead, and there is no doubt but what the Dodger's death hastened Sam's. These two were the slyest pair that I have ever met. I believe they understood each other's thoughts so well that when one's body itched the other could, without seeing his friend make a motion, scratch his own body at the exact place. These two conversed by looks, and uttered very few words. They were so well-matched and thought so much of one another, that something more than accident must have brought two such men together. It was always clear that if anything happened to part them, neither one would seek friendship elsewhere.

I had seen all these men fighting against death day after day, but with such determination, that I can hardly believe the report that calls them dead; especially as there is no proof of lettered stone, seeing that they are all in paupers' graves. All these poor invalids in common lodging-houses are under the impression that doctors, when they find that their patients have no friends, and cannot be thoroughly cured, kill them. That is why they are so stubborn, and fight till they cannot move, before they will enter a hospital.

Chapter XVIII

The Earnings of Beggars

In writing of the earnings of beggars, I do not, of course, include common tramps, who are satisfied with barns, sheds, empty houses and workhouses; I write of true beggars, who have not lost their self-respect, and who, by their exertions, are as sure of a bed at night—although it is a different one—as other people that have homes. If they sleep out of doors for a night or two in summer-time, they do so for pleasure; as people with homes will, when they sleep in hammocks under trees. The true beggar does not shirk business, or save money by sleeping out; he still follows his calling and makes the price of his bed, but in this instance he spends the money on ale instead of stifling with so many others in a common lodging-house.

A good beggar is always ready to seize opportunities. He will never allow a man to pass on who greets him pleasantly, or requires information, without either begging a copper, a pipeful of tobacco, or even a match. I think now of that memorable morning in America, when Brum, an excellent beggar, saw a lady kiss a horse. We were at a camp fire making coffee, when I was startled by the unusual eagerness of Brum's voice crying, "Look!" Following the direction of his finger, I saw a lonely house on a hill, and near the house was a lady in riding-habit, and she was patting a horse's neck. Seeing nothing unusual in this, I said, "What's the matter?" "You were too late to see," answered Brum; "she kissed the horse!" Now I am very fond of dumb creatures, and was therefore very pleased to see Brum moved so nobly by such an incident; but I was not allowed much time to congratulate myself on meeting with such a kind-hearted companion, for these were Brum's next words; "A lady that kisses a horse ought to be good for a piece of silver"; and before I could utter a word he had gone. This incident plainly shows how quick a good beggar is to take advantage of an opportunity. And Brum was right, for he not only returned with a piece of silver in his pocket, but also a parcel of food in his hand.

Of course, second-rate beggars in America earn more than first-rate beggars in Europe. In any of the large cities of America an active beggar can obtain as much as three dollars in a couple of hours, even if he suspends work for a drink. If a beggar is lucky enough to meet a gambler, he is just as likely to get a dollar as ten cents; in fact a number of beggars in that country make gambling places their haunts, for gamblers are well known to be superstitious, and few of them would think of refusing a beggar when on their way to the tables.

One of the quickest ways to make a good haul is to beg a fast overland train, when it must stop at some out-of-the-way place to take in water or coal. A beggar often boards one of these trains and, taking off his hat—not out of respect, but to hold money—goes from passenger to passenger, from one end of the train to the other. It is necessary to do business very quick, for the train does not stop long, and the conductor must be avoided. If a man has the luck to get right through the train, he often has several dollars to his account.

In this country beggars have different methods. No doubt singing hymns in Welsh towns and villages is one of the most profitable forms of begging. The Welsh are very kind-hearted and, being a musical people, it is almost impossible for them to resist an appeal made by song. When murder has been committed in a locality, you will always find a couple of men making a song of it in the streets, and they certainly do an excellent trade with their song-sheets. Good voices are not so necessary as a distinct enunciation of particular words such as blood, axe, bolster, etc. But even in less fortunate cases, when there has not even been an attempt at murder, beggars can still do well by singing well-known hymns.

There is one kind of beggar in Wales whose earnings can water the mouth of many a beggar in America. We must approach this man very seriously, for he is forced to beg through a terrible affliction. He is either totally blind or paralysed, and is to be seen standing or sitting near a pit's mouth on pay-day. For this man the Welsh colliers have deep pity, and in a very short time they fill his hat with money, silver shining among the copper, although the contributors are only working men. But for a man with a more simple affliction the colliers have, of course, far less sympathy. A great number of colliers have suffered in accidents, and they are still working hard, so it cannot be expected that they will make much distinction between a man who has lost a finger and one that has not.

Beggars that play music do well, whether it is an organ, a cornet, a concertina, or a tin whistle. Public-houses are the best stands, for men half drunk are always musically inclined. These men also do well at private houses. It seems strange to say that houses where a hungry man has difficulty in getting bread, can generally find a copper for a beggar musician. The reason is very simple: music pleases the children, and, naturally, a mother is always willing to assist men that make the children laugh and dance, and the baby bounce in her arm. In fact these men are not regarded as beggars, but entertainers. If they know their business well, they will keep a sharp eye on the door and windows, and when they see a child's face, nod and smile, and throw kisses to it. Then the child laughs and claps its little hands, and the mother hears the child and she laughs also. The meanest woman would not rob the child of this enjoyment, and if she allows the music to continue she is under a moral obligation to pay for it.

I knew Billy the whistler well, and he only had one complaint—dogs. He could seldom blow three notes on his tin whistle before he was accompanied, against his wish, by a dog's voice. The bottom of his trousers was always in tatters, so much did dogs dislike a tin whistle.

Manchester Jack was one of the best beggars that I have met in this country. He scorned to play music, sing, or sell. Although he was a big, strong, able-bodied man in the prime of life, he could earn more than a crippled young man or an old man feebled and paralysed. This sounds like a reproach to the world, but it is very easy to explain. Manchester Jack, being active and business-like, could call at three times more houses than a man that was afflicted by age or accident. He would certainly be refused at one or two places where the latter would succeed, but the greater number of houses he called at would give him the advantage. From a beggar's point of view, the world consists of two kinds of people—the good and the bad. The good will not refuse a man because he is able-bodied, and the bad can and will always find some excuse for not giving assistance. The very few that give in particular cases are in such a minority that a man like Manchester Jack would be very little affected.

I travelled with him for ten days, and when I took one side of a street, and he the other, he not only finished his side first, but, starting at the other end of mine, would meet me half way. He was a kind-hearted fellow, always willing to give strangers information about good or bad towns. On one occasion, when we had just finished begging a street, Manchester Jack asked me if I had received any scrand (food). I told him yes; that I had taken fivepence and two parcels of food, which were in my pockets. "Well, lad," he answered, "I have taken ninepence, but no scrand. Let me have the scrand and I will make it all right later on." I gave him the two parcels, but was considerably taken by surprise; for I knew Jack was too proud a beggar to be seen eating in public, and preferred to sit comfortably in a warm lodging-house kitchen. Taking the food he went to a house that he had just left, knocked at the door, handed in the parcels and began to retreat, followed by a woman's voice, which made him hurry faster. When he came back he explained to me that he had called at that house, and the woman had begun to cry, saying at last that she was in want herself. "So," said Manchester Jack, "I have given her your parcels and a couple of pennies to get a bit of tea."

On another occasion he was leaving a house when he ran into a very dirty-looking tramp, who was wasting his precious time looking at the doors instead of knocking at them. "Mister," said this dirty and timid man, judging Jack by his smart walk and confident smile to be the tenant of the house—"Mister," said he, "is the Mrs. any good for a mouthful of bread?" "Here," answered Jack, giving him a penny— "here, and get out of this street at once; for a beggar has just left this house, and the lady cannot give to everyone; take my advice and go to another street."

I got on very well with Manchester Jack, and we might have been together for a long time, had he not been arrested for begging, and sentenced to a few days' imprisonment.

Chapter XIX

Charity in Strange Quarters

A fine house is seldom worth a beggar's notice, for the simple reason that it has too many people to consult. The servant girl has to tell the cook, and the cook has her orders from the mistress; and either one of these has power to stop the flow of charity. The servant girl may, if no one is looking, dismiss a beggar with a shake of her head; or the cook may think she has quite enough work to do without waiting on tramps. The fact of the matter is that you can seldom find a servant and her mistress of one mind; if the latter is kind and charitable, it is often found that the servant is otherwise. If the mistress is mean and uncharitable, the servant is often—sometimes through spite, and no kindness in herself—inclined to charity. All tramps have experiences to relate of how kind-hearted ladies or gentlemen have come out of the house and called them back, or met them at the gate and, after enquiring their wants, led them back to the house and reprimanded the servants for sending poor men away empty-handed. Again, there are other cases of servant girls giving charity against the strict orders of their masters and mistresses—girls with good, kind hearts. So, you see, a fine house is so unreliable that it always pays a beggar to confine his efforts to small houses. There is not the least doubt but what bells cry hunger, common iron knockers spell charity, and shabby doors that cannot afford either bell or knocker, and require bare knuckles, are—from a beggar's point of view—the richest.

Even when rich people are charitable, and give food, clothes, and money, they never seem to be impressed by the word workhouse; for they seem to regard that place as a comfortable home. But to mention workhouse to the poor is to send a shudder through them, and they will always try to assist a man to escape it. They see that dreadful place before themselves, when old age and poverty come, and they pity a man that has to go there, if only for one night.

A man that played an accordion, whom I often saw, had a certain pitch. People that passed by could not help but pity him, thinking that he was a stranger in the town, and did not know the almshouses from other dwellings. But this musician knew well what the houses were, for he had been to them before and—in a whisper—these almshouses were almost his best pitch. Going up a narrow passage, he would take up a position in a large stone yard, where he would stand and play a few tunes, and would be rewarded with three or four pennies and a couple of parcels of food. This was certainly good, for it was all bunts (profit). He will not be so successful when he plays to a row of fine villas at the other end of the town. If it were not for making himself a nuisance, and being paid to go away, it would never be worth while to play to fine houses.

I shall never forget the summer's day when I accidentally discovered a long row of small houses hidden away from all eyes. Having been given a sandwich, I had put it in my pocket, but on second thoughts decided to wrap it in paper. Seeing a dark, narrow passage between two shops, I entered, so as to have some privacy to do so. While I was in the act of wrapping this sandwich in paper, and returning it to my pocket, I was surprised at being passed by three small children, and wondered what they were doing there. But I lost sight of them at once, around a short bend in the passage. Being curious to know what was around this bend, I advanced, and what do you think I saw? A long yard, with more than a dozen small cottages in a row. This was a lovely sight for a beggar! In there a man could beg without fear of policemen, and without being annoyed by the stares of people passing in carts and on foot. But the best of it was that these houses would escape ninety-nine beggars out of a hundred.

I lost no time in going to work, in spite of a number of children that were playing in the yard. Instead of beginning at the first house, as an amateur would, I passed them all by, intending to begin at the extreme end, calling at every house on my return. My motive for doing this will be approved by all true beggars; it was to advertise my presence, so that people would expect me, and save me the trouble of knocking and explaining my wants, and my time would not be wasted. This turned out well, for, after I had called at the end cottage, where I was not expected, I had nothing to do after but receive the ready pennies and food from the neighbours, as I came to them. As I have said, it was a summer's day, and all the doors were open, so that the people could hardly fail to know of my arrival. Moreover, the children had found time to run in and tell their mothers to expect me, and when. No beggar could ever have done business quicker, for in less than a quarter of an hour, I was finished, having received fivepence halfpenny and two parcels of food. At one house, where I was given a penny, the woman also gave me a glass of beer, saying that she was thirty-five years of age that day, and had been married fourteen years, and was respected wherever she went.

Yes, sometimes charity comes from strange quarters, as only beggars know. One day an old lady gave me half a chicken and a sponge cake, with the information that she was getting parish relief. I don't know how to account for this, but suppose she was fortunate in being well looked after by some rich family for whom she had worked.

Another time I went to a small cottage, and the door was answered by a very shabby-looking old lady. I was selling needles and laces, at the time, and, when the old lady was asked to buy, she answered that she had not one penny in the house. She looked so very poor that I felt ashamed of having called there, and felt much inclined to make her a present of a packet of needles. As I was about to leave, she said: "Would you like to have something to eat?" Not caring to take anything from this poor woman, I said: "No, thank you; I have plenty in my pockets." "No matter for that," she answered briskly. Saying this, she went indoors, and in a few moments returned with a brown-paper parcel in her hands. It looked very much like a suit of clothes, but when I received it I was astonished at its weight. Thanking her I left, and at the first opportunity sat down to examine the contents. To my surprise I had half a rabbit pie and a whole custard pudding. This woman, it seemed, was far from being poor, and lived well; and that she had not a penny in the house was not to say that she was in poverty, as I first supposed.

When I was once followed by school-children, I could not help but see by their whispers that something unusual was about to happen. It was not long before a little girl came forward and put a penny in my hand. This was the most extraordinary charity that I ever received; for the child was old enough to know the value of money and the number of sweet things, so dear to childhood, that a penny could buy. Another, a little boy, seeing this wonderful deed of sacrifice, wanted me to take his slice of bread and jam, most of the jam being licked off.

A beggar soon forgets a kindness, but it is most certain that the charity he receives from the young affects him longest. Sometimes boys, who take their dinners with them to work, have food left; and it gives them great pride to meet a beggar and give it to him. Sometimes—more often than not—it is only dry bread; and they offer it to a beggar who perhaps has better food in his pockets. Now, if a man or woman gave such a beggar this dry bread, he would most likely receive it with indifference and cold thanks, and throw it away, being none too particular in carrying it beyond the eyes of the giver. But when he is offered this dry bread by innocent, well-meaning boys, he not only takes it with a great show of gratitude and pleasure, but is very careful that the boys will get no chance to see him throw it away.

Chapter XX

Enemies of Beggars

It is almost time that our streets were cleared of so many house-callers that, hour after hour, knock at doors and ring bells until a lady is not in a fit condition to listen to a beggar. It is commonly thought that policemen and dogs are a beggar's only enemies, but this is far from true; even the child that waits at the gate to see if he gets anything, and, if possible, what he does get—even this small innocent must be regarded as an enemy to a beggar; not to mention hundreds of adults that pester people for rent and instalments for goods received, and others that beg people to buy coal, wood, and oil, vegetables and fruit. Of course, these callers do not matter much to the true beggar, for he goes blindly to work, careless of his surroundings; but the timid beginner, who looks to the right and left of him, before and behind, is very apt to pass on if a neighbourhood is not kept more quiet for his work.

The true beggar, as I have said, is not often annoyed by these pestilent callers. Sometimes he knocks at a door and, before his knock can be answered, some infernal agent comes to the same door. In a case of this kind, the new beggar would be flurried, and most likely leave the house in possession of his enemy—but it is far different with the true beggar. He wishes his enemy a cheerful good morning—although it is seldom that he gets a civil answer—and is not afraid to speak out when the lady comes. In fact, he would be the first to explain his business, whether he was there first or not.

A first-class beggar like Brum would scorn to mention such little difficulties as these, and I know well that all good beggars will despise me for raising such paltry objections. But even Brum himself has given way before people that were not regarded as beggars; even he had to give way—not out of spite or ill-will, but through his kindness or generosity. One day, when we were both out begging, Brum surprised me with these words—"One beggar is quite enough in this street; let us go to another." I was quite surprised at these words, for I knew well that Brum would not have budged an inch if there were a dozen beggars in the street. But what surprised me more was that when I looked before and behind, I could not see anyone that could be mistaken for a beggar. "I don't see anyone," I said at last, looking at him for an explanation. "Don't you?" he asked. "Well, there she is, and good luck to her!" And to my astonishment he nodded towards a Sister of Charity. It would never have occurred to me to regard such a person as a beggar, but she certainly was; and it proved how kind-hearted and considerate Brum was to give way to her, so that she might have every opportunity to get what the street was worth.

I ought not to have been surprised to hear Brum say these words, for I had often heard him at the camps and elsewhere laud a certain Christian leader as "the greatest beggar that ever lived." To Brum this man was a perfect hero, whose prowess amazed him. Brum followed his career with as much interest as any man ever followed the doings of Napoleon; and every scrap of paper that came to hand, on which he saw the name of this Christian leader, was read and re-read by Brum, and commented on daily. In fact, Brum was never without two or three pieces of paper relating to "the greatest beggar that ever lived." "He does not beg a needle, a piece of thread, a cake, a sandwich, a pair of stockings, or a shirt," Brum would say, glancing with scorn at other beggars in the camp; "he knows nothing about our petty ways of doing business: he begs shiploads of provisions, wardrobes of clothes; aye, acres of land and barrels of money. And this man is an Englishman," Brum would add, with a slight sneer at any American beggars who happened to be present. The latter had to admit that their country had not yet produced so great a beggar.

Curly Jack, of England, had never met Brum and never heard of him, but he was of exactly the same opinion; but whereas Brum admired the man as a hero, Curly Jack abused him for his success. Whereas Brum was as delighted as a child to see his hero's banner in charge of a trusty officer, and to hear the band—Curly Jack no sooner saw or heard, than he slunk off in an opposite direction, scowling and muttering curses.

One Sunday morning Curly Jack and myself were in Northampton, and we had left the lodging-house together; after which we parted, he going down one street, while I went farther on, so as to give him plenty of room.

I did not find Northampton very bad, although the boot trade—its main industry—had been declining for a long time. In about half an hour I had several pennies over my bed money, also a quantity of food, so I thought I would get a newspaper and return to the lodging-house, and take it easy for the rest of the day.

As I was on my way back I saw Curly Jack going to a house, and waited—at his motion—until he was at liberty to come. "What luck, Jack?" I asked, when he came. "Very bad," he answered; "I was in a good street, where I have done well before, but twenty or thirty beggars have been there this morning before me, and played it out." These words surprised me not a little, and I asked him for an explanation. "There they are again," he cried, with an oath. I looked in every direction, but all I saw was three little children together, and one couple that appeared to be lovers. "Can't you hear the beggars?" he asked. "I hear the Salvation Army," I said; "surely you don't mean them!" "Of course I mean them," he answered, with some impatience. "What difference can they make?" I said, at a loss to understand him. "I should think their presence would be good for beggars—that they would open people's hearts." "Come with me, and I will show you how they spoil the street for a beggar," said Jack. And away we went.

In a few moments we were in the same street as the Salvation Army, and my companion walked boldly towards them, while I lingered a little behind. However, when I saw him standing near them, I joined him, and could not help but notice that several members of the Army rewarded our presence with smiles.

It was not long before I saw how the Salvation Army could spoil a street for a beggar. While the meeting was going on, several members not only went from house to house, but even begged passers-by—aye, even came to me and my seedy friend. "Now," said Curly Jack, as we were leaving—"now, are you satisfied? What chance has a beggar, be he ever so good, against these people? It will be impossible for the rest of the day to get a single penny in this street, or any other street that they have been to."

People will now be able to see, by these incidents, the great number of enemies a poor beggar has to contend with; enemies that would take the bread out of his mouth.

It is very true that in the green country beggars have a little dread of policemen and dogs, but in towns they fear more the annoyance of other callers, who are not beggars. One thing they dread very much, in towns of some size, is to be offered a ticket to introduce them to a charitable organization that professes to attend to their wants. True beggars know well what these organizations are. But sometimes the man who is looking for work is only too glad to receive this ticket—and he certainly gets plenty of work. He does about three shillings' worth of labour for a bed whose only virtue is cleanliness, and about threepenny worth of food. However, the poor fellow is well satisfied, because he is a very timid man, and he feels less shame in being made a slave than a beggar. He is only too glad to perform these tasks at every opportunity, but the true English beggar is a Briton that never will be a slave.

Chapter XXI

The Lowest State of Man

Some people think that a man cannot fall lower than to live in a common lodging-house; but men and women are occasionally met in London that are even stared at and pitied by those who live in such low places. The men and women of whom I speak would not be admitted into the lowest common lodging-houses in London. They are so ragged and filthy in appearance that if you gave one of them a sovereign it would be impossible to get a bed until an alteration was made in his or her appearance. Some of these have slept in their clothes so often and been outcasts so long that they are really without the least hope—not dejected for a few hours or days, as with others. Their dreams, if they have any, are recollections of days gone, but they have no hope in the future. Who has not seen them? Men and women in such a condition that if a man gives them a penny he has to avert his eyes; and the most kind-hearted women pass them by with as quick a glance as possible. There is only one place open to these poor wretches, and that is a Salvation Army shelter, where they pay twopence and sleep on the floor. They think nothing of suffering; one of them will sit on a seat, when it is raining hard, with the utmost indifference, and there may be an arch that he could reach in less than two minutes. So he gets wet and shivers all night, which is common for him.

I have seen a man of this description refused a bed at a Salvation Army lodging-house, and it did not take the officer many seconds to come to that conclusion. Of course, it is not often—perhaps half a dozen times in a year—that one of these poor people can afford to pay fourpence for a bed; but sometimes they have the good fortune to find a silver coin, or some gentleman gives it to them. If the latter is the case, the gentleman is probably a stranger in London, and comes from some happy new land where such extreme poverty is not known. One night, when I was at the office paying for my bed, I heard a man come in at the front door and stand behind me, but did not turn my head, thinking that he was one of the many lodgers that lived there. When I was about to leave I heard this man put down some money and tell the lieutenant that he wanted a bed. As I did not hear that officer make any answer, but rise from his stool instead to come out of the office, I turned my head, thinking something strange was about to happen. The lieutenant was soon out and standing before the would-be lodger, looking at him from head to foot. "I should think not," he said at last with an amused smile to think that the man had asked such a question. "We have no bed for you," he continued; "you had better go to the shelter in Blackfriars." The man was certainly a pitiful, even disgusting, sight. His hair was very long, and so was his beard; and the colour of his hands, his neck, and the hairless part of his face was almost black. His clothes were in tatters, showing his naked legs; his boots had no soles or heels, and the uppers were kept together with string. This poor fellow had either found a silver coin or had received it in charity; and, having slept in his clothes for months, he wanted them off for one night and the luxury of a warm bed. Not only that, but if this man had a bed, he would also have the use of the washhouse all the next day, with plenty of hot water to clean himself. But this was not to be, for the lieutenant was too keen-eyed. This poor fellow, who was so ambitious, did not seem at all surprised at the refusal, but picked up his money and walked out without a word. Perhaps he had been to other places with the same result, and would still go to others. The Christian officer watched him going, and, when he was gone, turned to re-enter his office. Seeing me standing there, a witness to what had happened, he said, "What a face!" and entered the office laughing—he, he, he!

Any person in London can see these poor wretches, who are in as low a state as it is possible to fall into. It is almost impossible to miss them, whether they are seated or walking, for if you are not looking their way you are almost certain of hearing strange sounds and having your attention drawn to them. They all talk to themselves, and laugh and swear; for cold nights and hunger have made them crazy to a great extent. Two of them are seldom seen together, for each one has just enough sense to know that he draws more attention than is good, without inviting more. Time is nothing to these; if they have enough bread to last the day, they are not likely to leave one particular seat. As a rule each one has a certain spot to spend the day, and, after being forced to walk all night, they return as soon as possible to their favourite place. It is in the early morning that they get their food, and where they get it is a secret each one keeps to himself. This secret is their living, and that is another cause why they should be reserved with one another. One of these men told me once that he knew a certain large private house where a paper parcel consisting of fragments of food was to be found every morning in the back alley, close to the ash-bin. This paper parcel had kept him for three years, but he had missed it several times. No doubt some stray beggar had found it on those occasions, but, not knowing that such a parcel was put there every morning, had never troubled to look for it again. When I heard this I could not help thinking how likely it was that something would happen to disappoint him; that the tenant's absence or death would alter such an arrangement. But I did not give the least hint of this, for I saw that the poor fellow thought he was sure of bread for life. He had not the least doubt but what the parcel would always be put there, and his only worry was that some other beggar would follow him and learn his secret, or discover the parcel by accident. In the winter this man spent all his days on one particular seat, when he could get it, and as near to it as possible when it was already taken. When I walked along the Embankment one morning, at nine o'clock, he was then seating himself. He had his paper parcel beside him, from which he had just taken a crust of bread. When I came back that way, at four o'clock in the afternoon, he was still there. Perhaps he would have a certain shady tree in one of the parks for his summer days.

None of these are beggars; they never go to houses or beg of people in the street, for they know that their appearance is so bad that they dare not draw more attention than people like to give them. Sometimes, not very often, a man has the courage to give them a coin, but no woman ever has. They are so surprised at receiving unsolicited charity that they forget to offer any thanks. The man whom I have just mentioned, who had a parcel of food every morning, would rather you passed him by without giving him money, for fear a policeman would see the act and accuse him of begging, and move him from his favourite seat. As I have said, most of them know places where they can get food without begging, outside large factories and elsewhere. They are seldom to be seen in private streets, because they do not beg houses.

I have often seen men standing outside large factories and workshops, waiting for the workmen, so as to get the food some of them have left from dinner and, being frugal husbands, are taking home; but who gladly give it to a man who they think wants it. These beggars generally ask a workman, when they see him with his food-tin, if he has anything left from dinner. Whether he has or not does not matter, for the question draws the attention of those that have, and in a few moments the beggar has enough for a couple of good meals. But these poor wretches, who have fallen so low in their appearance, have no need to speak at all, only to show themselves. For it is not only apparent to every eye that they are homeless, but it almost seems as if they never had homes. Such men are the only thorough outcasts, for whom nothing can be done. Neither the Salvation Army nor the Church Army will deal with them. And if one of these men went to the Charity Organization he would not be admitted inside the doors, much less receive the honour of being invited in and questioned. That particular Society would not be interested as to what his father did for a living or his grandfather's habits. In fact it does not need those hard, smart, detective qualities of charity officers to see that the date of social respectability must go back a very long way indeed in this man's past.

Chapter XXII

The Lodger Lover

A lodger gave him the name of "Cinders," and he took to it kindly. I was present in the kitchen on the day he arrived as a stranger, nameless and alone, as far as the other lodgers were concerned, for they did not know what name he had entered at the office. He was in rags and tatters, and "Rags" or "Tatters" should certainly have been his name. In fact the name was offered to him, but he returned an unsatisfactory stare. He was preparing his tea at the same table as "Punch," and the latter being in need of a pinch of salt, and seeing none of his friends at tea, asked this stranger to oblige him, saying: "Would you oblige me, 'Rags,' with a pinch of salt?" The man stared at "Punch" for a moment, and then walked away without giving an answer. He was at that time cooking a herring at the fire. Now it so happened that a few moments later this man was pouring out tea, when all at once there was a loud cry of "Whose herring is this?" The man turned quickly at the sound, and beheld his herring making a few spasmodic motions, as it dangled on a long wire. He immediately ran to the rescue, but alas! too late; for the tatters of his loose clothes encompassed him like a deadly plant, and when he arrived the herring was lying motionless under the grate. After great care he succeeded in bringing it to the light, covered with ashes and cinders. Still, with great care, he washed it and, after placing it flat on a plate, returned it to the fire. "I hope you do not blame me for that accident, 'Cinders,'" said kind-hearted "Punch." "Oh, no," answered the man newly named "Cinders." "'Cinders' has too much sense for that," said "Red-Nosed Scotty," who happened to be sitting near. "Whose teapot is this?" cried the kitchen-man, who was about to build the coke fire, and wanted all food and teapots removed. "It belongs to 'Cinders,'" said a number of voices. From that day to this his name is "Cinders," owing to the accident to his herring when he first came. If he was arrested, it would be—"'Cinders' is in jail"; and if he died it would be—"'Cinders' is dead."

If a man who goes to live in a common lodging-house does not utter his own name in a very short time, the lodgers will give him one. Brown had a large nose, and would most certainly have been named "Nosey," had he not on the first day recorded a simple anecdote of his childhood, in which he had cause to call himself William Brown.

I remember the day well, when the "Dodger"—a man who gladly helped others to spend their earnings on ale and, when they sat penniless and hungry, sat himself down alone to beefsteak and onions—I remember the day well when this man caused a never-to-be-forgotten sensation in the lodging-house kitchen. A letter was at the office for Algernon Dudley, and the manager had been in the kitchen several times in quest of that gentleman. It was near seven o'clock in the evening when he came into the kitchen for the fifth time and cried—"Is Algernon Dudley here?" "Yes," answered a man in the corner, and coming quickly forward. All eyes turned towards him, and who do you think Algernon Dudley was? No other than the common "Dodger." "Fatty," who claimed to be a fighting man, whom no man had ever succeeded in knocking down, said, in conversation to Brown, "You could have knocked me down with a feather."

Brown's remarks on this occasion were very sensible, as they usually were. "It was, is, and always will be the custom," said he, "for a woman that gives birth to a child to name it. For this reason she is no sooner on the trot again than she begins scheming to that end. Now," continued Brown, "we must not picture the 'Dodger' as he is—God help him!—but as he was, a child in the arms of a doting woman. Such was the case, and has been the same with others, including ourselves, and will always be. Now this poor woman—some people would call her foolish—no doubt had great respect for the 'Dodger' as a babe and, to distinguish him from the common race of mankind, named him in such a manner as we have just heard. Perhaps I am right, perhaps I am wrong; but if the true facts of the case were known, you would probably find that I was not far from the truth. In spite of all this, I quite agree with our friend's remark, that it fills us with astonishment." The "Dodger" had lived in the house for more than two years, when this incident caused so many comments.

But let us return to the man "Cinders," for that gentleman was no helpless wreck in a doss-house; he was really a gay spirit and capable of love. He was a man with a long, melancholy face, seeing no humour in life and, if the truth must be told, he was positively ugly. Yet this man "Cinders" had been seen on several occasions walking the streets with a woman on his arm. One of the lodgers said her looks were passable, and another said that they were more than passable compared to "Cinders." Brown had seen them together and, said he, "Although a man ought to believe his own eyes, I would never believe such to be the case, had not 'Cinders' said, 'Good night, Mr. Brown.' And if a man is not to believe both eyes and ears, then what is he to believe?"

Of course, there could be no union between these poor souls; for she was in service, and he did odd jobs at the market, earning a shilling, or a little more on lucky days. As the manager said, it was amusing and could not amount to anything serious. They could go on walking arm in arm all their lives, for they would never be able to marry and walk apart.

This courtship had been the talk of the house for over three months when, one night, it was brought to an end in a strange manner. "Cinders" and his love had been all the evening in the "Borough" drinking ale. He, seeing some smoked haddock, fancied some for his supper and, after making a purchase, rejoined his fair companion. It was near midnight when it suddenly occurred to "Cinders" that the manager closed the house at twelve p.m., and if he—"Cinders"—was not there by that time, he would be out for the night. Reminding his lady of this, they both started for home, her road lying the same way as his. The manager was just closing the door when "Cinders" arrived.

Now, goodness knows what demon put it into this woman's head to cook her lover's fish, but this she seemed determined to do. "I am coming in to cook your supper," said she. "No," said the manager, "this is a house for men only, and we do not allow women to enter. Not only that, the kitchen is now closed, and I would not open it again for 'Cinders' or any other man. He will have to go supperless to bed, or seek lodgings elsewhere." The lady then started to abuse the manager in a loud voice, but that gentleman, not heeding her, caught "Cinders" by the shoulders, saying, "Go to bed, you old fool," at the same time shutting the door in the lady's face.

The next morning, when "Cinders" was cooking his haddock, the manager lectured him severely on what had occurred the previous night; telling him that if he could afford to keep a lady cook he must seek better lodgings. Brown, who happened to be within hearing, gave evidence that he distinctly heard a woman's voice say, "I am going to cook his fish," but thought he must be dreaming. Even now he believed it was all a dream, and he would like to hear the truth from the manager's own lips, as to whether it was an actual fact or not. On being told that it was, Brown turned his eyes towards "Cinders" and, seeing that gentleman hold down his head in wordless shame, Brown was forced to believe it all. Probably that was the end of their courtship, for they were never seen together after that.

Chapter XXIII

The Handy Man

The handy man is to be found in all places where men are either too poor to pay for professional experience, or, not being so poor, yet live in out-of-the-way camps which women have never visited, and which are too temporary for tradesmen to open business. The former places are common lodging-houses, where the handy man volunteers his services as laundryman, cook, tailor, cobbler, barber, etc. In fact, according to his boasted qualifications, it would be far more interesting to learn what he cannot do than what he can. He has learnt all these trades with his eye, and, when about to practise, his confidence is unshaken. Says he, "I will shave you, and you will not feel the razor going over your face." And when he covers your face with blood he blames pimples, which you never had, and expects to be thanked for removing them; for in addition to shaving you, has he not also performed a successful surgical operation?

In this manner he earns a shilling or more a day, and he is not agreeable that any man should shave himself, sew or wash clothes; or he would not earn the price of his bed and board, and gifts of ale and tobacco. If he sees me preparing to shave, he makes a rush and possesses himself of the razor, and commands me to be seated. There is nothing else to do but obey, for he takes me by the shoulder and leads me to a seat; he then forces me down and pushes my head back until it is within an inch of the nape of my neck. For this indignity I give him a penny, and then, while I am washing, he shouts in a loud voice—"Next." He never thinks that I would object to my soap, brush, and razor being used on other faces; and truly it is for that reason—and not economy—that I shave myself. But thank goodness the kitchen is almost empty, and there is no answer to his "Next." Then, with an eye to future custom, he carefully wipes the razor, dries it on his clothes, washes the brush, rolls the soap in a piece of clean paper, and returns them to the owner. After which he again borrows the razor, for he has seen a hair on the throat, and, as he says—"A good craftsman likes to make a neat job." He then laments the number of pimples that had to be removed, and wanders in quest of other jobs.

Probably he now sees a man in the act of repairing a boot. If he does, he rushes in that direction, wrestles with the man for the boot, and is soon heard hammering with all his might. He makes so much noise that any man would think him a man of confidence and great practice. Of course he blames the tools for every mistake, and says modestly that no man living could do better under such conditions. For rendering this assistance he receives two or more coppers.

And now he sees a man whose eyesight is bad endeavouring to thread a needle. "Allow me," cries the handy man, springing forward, and wrestling with the other for the needle and thread. Getting possession of these, in spite of the other's loud-spoken annoyance, he, instead of returning them, demands the article to be sewn. "No, thank you," says the other; "I can manage it myself." With much reluctance the handy man surrenders, and begs a pipeful of tobacco for threading the needle. But he still keeps his eye on the other, and when he sees him take up a shirt and a patch, the handy man again springs forward and in a loud voice commands the other to halt. "I," says he, "have a piece of stuff that exactly matches your shirt, whereas yours is far different." Snatching the shirt from the other's hand, he disappears for a moment, and then reappears with a piece of stuff that, it must be admitted, is a better match. The other, being well pleased at this, says: "If you don't mind waiting we will have a drink after I have done this job." The handy man, hearing this, and not feeling inclined to wait long, also thinking that an additional kindness would meet its reward in an additional drink, answers: "You had better let me do it, for by the way you hold the needle it is plain that you are not used to such work." The other, seeing that he has already given tobacco, and is compromised for a drink, is now quite willing to have the handy man's assistance. "Now," says he, when the job is done, where every stitch is seen to lie in its own deep valley surrounded by hills—"Now," says he, "all it requires is to be pressed with a hot flat-iron, after which you need not be ashamed to show it to the best tailor in the land. If you like, we will use the interval, while the iron is in the fire, for refreshment."

The handy man, though he often spoils good things which, with a little professional care, might be made almost as good as new, is not to be altogether despised. Though he is not the handy man of his claim, he certainly deserves credit for keeping handy tools. Wherever he finds discarded boots or clothes, he cuts patches and saves them for emergency. He always keeps a pair of scissors, a razor, strap, brush, pincers, and many other useful things, and he is seldom short of nails. But to one who is determined to do without his services, he is often a very unpleasant spectator. For instance, if I am shaving the handy man stands two feet away, glaring like a discomforted demon; and when I stand before the glass, and the razor is on my face, he stands behind my back, so that to my confusion and danger two faces are reflected. If he sees a man who has persistently declined his aid, and who is in the act of sewing, the handy man either stands in the light, or stands seemingly counting the stitches, critically watching, until the man must either prick his finger or spoil his work. When he sees a man repairing a boot he says sarcastically: "Take care you strike the right nail." The other laughs, but proves his confusion when the next instant he strikes off the nail of his left-hand thumb.

The handy man even prescribes for the sick, but in nine cases out of ten his cure is an intoxicant, the time being immaterial. I allowed him to cut my hair, and he seemed well pleased at the result; but after one glance in the glass, I decided not to remove my cap for three weeks, whether at meals or not.

Perhaps nothing worse could befall a house than to have two rival handy men. I was at one place where a man claimed to have given satisfaction for a number of years. He was certainly liked, for even those who scorned his talents could not resist his ways as a cadger of tea, sugar, tobacco, and other things. But alas! his fatal day came when a man, who was receiving a good pension, took lodgings at the same house, and, wanting something to occupy his mind, began shaving, cutting hair, and mending boots free of charge. "Look here," said the old handy man to the new one—"Look here, before you came I could always pay for my bed, tobacco, not to mention a glass or two of ale; but your coming here has spoilt all that." "Well," answered the good-natured pensioner, "you are one of the biggest and strongest men in the house, and why don't you look for a man's labour, instead of loafing about for a woman's work— sewing and washing clothes? I am not taking pennies from poor fellows old or broken in health who as paper-men, toy-sellers, and sandwichmen, barely earn enough for their own wants." Not many days after this the big, healthy schemer had to walk out for his living, and had heavy tasks put before him, which he was well able to perform. Then the poor lodgers had peace to do their own washing and mending, while the good-natured pensioner attended to their boots, beard, and hair.

Chapter XXIV

On Books

I have never had much chance to enjoy books. Even after writing four books, which were regarded as literary successes, my library consisted of only about fifty volumes, some of which were magazines, and not worth a second reading. This being so, it is hardly likely that I can ever forgive this world for keeping me without books when my enthusiasm was great, for I don't want them now. I have often envied the thousands of rich people that have well-stocked libraries and no desire to use them. When my enthusiasm was greatest I was not able to enjoy books owing to the circumstances under which they had to be read. For instance, when I lived in a common lodging-house, preferring freedom on a small income to drudgery on a large one, I had plenty of time to visit free libraries. At those places I could, by signing my name and address, borrow any book mentioned in the catalogue, and read it on the premises. I often wish I now had some of the books I read at that time and could not enjoy. The reason I could not enjoy them at that time was owing to several causes, which were strong enemies against enthusiasm. In the first place, I had to give a false address, because the name of a lodging-house was not respectable, and condemned me as unclean. Owing to this I could never feel comfortable, for if I happened to look up from my book and saw the librarian looking my way, I always thought that he was weighing in his mind what manner of man I was. Sometimes a librarian would stare at me so boldly that

I lost no time in returning the book, and leaving the place, thinking that he would soon come forward and tell me to do so. Of course, I was very suspicious, under those circumstances, but have often thought since that those men were not thinking of me at all, but were lost in their own business, and did not know what their eyes were doing. Another reason why I could not enjoy books then was owing to a low and insufficient diet, which kept my blood too cold to sit long in a room where the windows were often wide open. The consequence was that I often returned a very interesting book after an hour's reading, so as to take a walk and get warm; a book which would, if I had a cosy little room of my own, be read through at one sitting, though it took far into the night. And when summer came, I wanted to read in the open air, but had no friends to recommend me as a book-borrower. For that reason I could not borrow books to take away and read at my leisure, and in whatever place I liked.

Since those days, and now that I have made one or two friends, I have other reasons to spoil my enjoyment of books. I cannot now read with enjoyment books that are borrowed or are likely to be wanted back. Such books are never any good to me, for, if I enjoy them, I am robbed of that joy by the thought that they are not mine. I want to see the books around me as my own property, else the sight of them grieves me. My own books are kept on a shelf, and I look on them as pure thoroughbred; but I keep apart all borrowed books, treating them as wandering mongrels to whom I have given a temporary home, and am as anxious to drive away as I was to receive them in the beginning. For this reason I would not now take advantage of a library, even if it were next door.

Unfortunately, in the country a book lover has to be well off, for he can only buy new books; whereas in London, and other large cities, a man can take, from stalls of second-hand books, an armful of classics for the price of a moderate meal. And that leads me to another thought—I do not care for the look of new books, much preferring them to have lost their last coat of polish. Somehow it hurts my conscience to see a dear old author shining before me in gold and spotless green or red. I seem to hear his voice say: "You scorned my coming in years past, and left me for these late and colder days." There is not much excuse for a man living in London not having a good stock of books. I have seen Shakespeare for fourpence, and Milton for half that price. At this rate a man could in a few months have a large stock of good books, and the outlay would not be much. If I had been living in London during these last two years, my books would now run into several hundreds, and I would not have spent five pounds.

Perhaps one of the best week's enjoyment I have ever had was in the free library at Reading, in spite of the conditions under which I then lived. I had left London three months before, and had been wandering about the country, and had not read a book or magazine during all that time. At this time I was aching with all my heart for reading matter, dreaming of books day and night. Now it happened that I had been in that town two months before, and on that occasion had been in the library long enough to see that it was very comfortable and had a good stock of papers and magazines. For, being a large town, that library was really free, without any signs relating to tramps—as I had seen in smaller towns—silence only being requested. Unfortunately, the town's trade was very bad at this time, and for that reason it would take me all day to sell enough laces to keep me, and I would have no spare time for the library. So I left Reading, with much regret, but determined to return if I could make a few shillings to keep me idle for several days. One Friday night I happened to be at Windsor and heard a couple of beggars in the lodging-house speaking in good terms of Slough, a mile and a half away. So, the next morning, being Saturday, I left Windsor and started for Slough. When I reached that town, I began to knock at doors without wasting any time, although it was quite early in the day, for some of the better-class people had not yet cleared away their breakfast things. I certainly had extraordinary luck, for I took a shilling before dinner and, of course, the town would be much better after that, because of the men having come home with their pay. To understand my good fortune people must know that Saturday morning is the worst time in the week for a beggar. It is so bad that nine beggars out of ten attempt no business whatever until after dinner, so as not to spoil themselves by being refused at good houses that would gladly assist them later in the day. It is really surprising the number of poor people there are who have spent the last penny in the house on a Saturday morning before dinner. When I thought of this it suddenly occurred to me that Reading library was not far away. No sooner had this idea occurred to me than I made up my mind to keep calling at houses until I had four shillings. It was getting dark, and must have been about five o'clock, when I stopped and counted a pocketful of pennies. First of all I counted my laces, and found that I had sold a dozen pairs, which had cost me threepence. But so many people had given pennies for nothing that I was not at all surprised to find that I had four shillings and tenpence, although one lady had insisted on having two pairs for three-halfpence. In addition to this money I had food enough given me for tea that night and breakfast the following morning. I was quite delighted at this and started at once for Maidenhead, four miles away. On the road there I sold three pairs of laces to men going home from work, and also had threepence given me by a gentleman taking a walk, which was unsolicited. So that I now had five shillings and fourpence, a clear five shillings after paying for my bed at Maidenhead. The next day, being Sunday, I walked with a light heart into Reading, with five shillings in my pocket. That small amount kept me for six days, and I never did, and never will again, have so much enjoyment out of reading matter. Of course, what increased my pleasure was the thought that I was letting a small income accumulate, so as to publish a book of my own; the manuscript was in my pocket then, and in two more months I would be an author.

Chapter XXV

Narks

A man cannot be a very long time on the road before he understands the meaning of the word "narks." Beggars may forgive dirty beds, vermin, broken crockery and bad fires, but to tell them that a lodging-house is full of "narks" is the worst information that can be conveyed to them. When I enquired of a beggar as to the comfort of the lodging-house in the town to which I was going, he said: "Well, mate, the bed is good, and a good fire is kept, but to tell you the truth the house is spoilt by 'narks.'" As I was not an old traveller in England, I did not understand him, but thought I would find out for myself what a "nark" really was.

After I had reached the town, and paid the lodging-house keeper for my bed, I entered the lodgers' kitchen, and there saw three men seated before a good fire. Of my cheerful "Good afternoon," they took not the least notice, neither did they offer to make room for a stranger coming in out of the cold. I could see at once by this that they were not true beggars and travellers, who are always eager to make room for their fellows. I may as well say at once that these three men were "narks." In other words, they were town beggars; men that had lost their homes and had to take refuge in a common lodging-house; or, if they did not belong to the town, they had been there long enough to be known.

The "nark" is either a cattle-drover, a small hawker, a mechanic that only has a couple of days' work a week, or a man that earns a few pennies by doing odd jobs for people that know him. Sometimes he is a man with a very small pension or income, and does nothing. Although the lodging-house keeper often abuses him, and threatens to cast him adrift, for all that he is allowed privileges which the casual wandering tramp cannot like. All true wanderers hate him; even the drunken, domineering grinder is treated with civility in a house where beggars see a "nark."

That the "nark," with his mean tricks, is a nuisance to wandering beggars is seen in a very short time. For instance, he takes the utensils, which are meant for the common use of the kitchen, and after using them will hide them away for his own future use; so that strangers have often to make tea in a pot without a spout, and look in vain for a saucer or a small saucepan. He also monopolizes the fire with newly-washed clothes, and hungry strangers find great difficulty in cooking their food. He will not oblige by removing these things until the evening, when there would be less demand for the fire. Again, he wants a certain place at the table to sit and eat his food, and he often frowns at innocent strangers who are enjoying their meal in his accustomed seat. He is often mean enough to allow his things to remain on the table after he has done, in readiness for the next meal—instead of clearing them away and making room for hungry new-comers.

The worst charge to make against a "nark" is that he is a spy and a tell-tale, and that he lets the lodging-house keeper know all the transactions of the kitchen. When lodgers are told the next morning that they cannot have a bed at that house for another night, and cannot get to know the reason why, they come to the conclusion that they have been reported by a "nark" for complaining about a bad fire, insufficiency of bed-clothes, teapots, saucers, or cups.

Most deputies in lodging-houses were in the first place "narks." Sometimes a "nark" fails, in spite of being well known in the town, to earn the price of his bed, or to borrow it, and returns to the lodging-house for trust. After that he shows his gratitude by sweeping the kitchen, or washing plates and tea-things, which the lodging-house keeper had to do himself. The latter, seeing this, asks him to do other things, and of course gives him bed and board, and a shilling at the end of the week. He no longer goes out as a drover, or seeking odd jobs, but sweeps, washes, scrubs, makes beds, etc. Taking everything into consideration the work is not so unremunerative as it appears, for every man in the house solicits his friendship. From morning till night he is offered saucers-full of tea from the many lodgers. In fact, he is often at his wits' end to know how to spend his very small wages, for the lodgers supply him with tobacco, beer, and even clothes and boots. He gets so many presents every week that he makes money by selling them.

As may be expected, it is from the "narks" that he reaps the most profit; for they never fail to share with him their titbits and give him the price of beer, which makes him favour that class, and prejudiced against casual lodgers.

Unfortunately the deputy has great power, against which there is no appeal. He will allow a "nark" to cook on the fire until it is nearly out; but when he sees a stranger cooking he will interfere, saying that the fire must be attended to. After which he will put on so much coke that the poor stranger is delayed an hour or more in doing what he has perhaps half done. He has to put on one side a herring half cooked, or a singing kettle, until the fire burns.

It is a good policy for strangers, as soon as they enter a lodging-house kitchen, to not only speak pleasantly to the deputy, but to slip a penny into his hand, so that they may be installed on an equal footing with "narks." Men that do not think of doing this must not be surprised if he "accidentally" overturns their teapots, or shovels coke into their frying-pans. These little accidents always add to the gaiety of "narks," and they the more generously reward the deputy for affording them this extra entertainment.

I was in one lodging-house in the provinces that only had accommodation for twelve lodgers, and in that house were six "narks" and the deputy. The night I was there, there were only three strangers, myself and two others, and we were almost afraid to move. One "nark" was a rag-and-bone man, who worked the country for miles around. While I was eating my frugal supper, he spread on the table his dirty rags and bones—so near that one bone was found on my plate, which I returned to him—with many thanks. Seeing that the deputy appeared quite satisfied, I dared not say much, for if I got into trouble and had my money returned, there was not another lodging-house within six miles.

Another "nark" was a drunken drover, who left a saucepan on the fire while he went out for a drink. When he returned he said that there were only four potatoes and a half in the saucepan, whereas he had put in five. It never occurred to his suspicious mind that one potato had become small in the extra boiling, and we three strangers had to tolerate his savage looks.

Another "nark" was a blacksmith, who was out of work. This man was lying drunk at full length on a bench, so that the two strangers had to wait until I had finished my meal before they could get a seat at the table, for, with the exception of the drover, all the other "narks" had had their supper.

The blacksmith had not paid his rent for two or three nights, and the landlady—a very old woman—had ordered the deputy not to allow him to go to bed. While I was asleep that night, I was suddenly awaked by a slap on the face, and a croaking voice, which said—"Out of my house, blacksmith." When I opened my eyes, I saw an old withered face bending over mine—there must have been a hundred years in that face. "I am not the blacksmith," I said feebly. "Liar," she shrieked, holding the candle near my face. However, she saw her mistake, and went away muttering, without making any apology for her mistake. No stranger would ever think of staying two nights in a house like that.

Of course, in a house where there is only one "nark," he tries to ingratiate himself with casual men, for the sake of social company, but they do not encourage his advances, knowing how careful they must be of what they say. They are suspicious of him, in spite of his good-natured offers to oblige them with a shake of pepper. By the way, the sight of a pepper-box in a lodging-house kitchen is always a sure sign that the man behind it is a "nark." Wanderers, however much trouble they take to carry tea, salt, soap, thread, needle, comb, and many other little things which must not interfere with space for food—would never think of carrying a pepper-box, though they may carry a little pepper in paper.

No, a "nark" is not a desirable companion, and to inform a tramp that he is going to a house that is full of them, is to daunt him more than to say that the teapots are spoutless and cracked, the saucers have no rims, the beds are dirty, and that the fire is small and often out.

Chapter XXVI

The Scribe in a Lodging-house

A man who is seen writing in a common lodging-house will soon have his services sought so often that he must be offended, however kind-hearted he may be. He will be pestered by illiterate seekers of work, and even begging-letter impostors. In the latter case the men are cunning enough to invent pitiful tales, but they lack the education to write them. Many a man who has only lived a short time in a lodging-house, and is innocent of the world, has written letters for these rogues, and not known what he was doing. Strange to say, very few of these men are able to write their own letters; and, seeing that they usually pose for men that have lost good positions, it is not to be wondered at when they have no courage to face a personal interview. With regard to honest seekers of work, a man will soon be sorry that he has obliged them, because of the awkward position in which it places him. For instance, if they do not receive any answer to your letter, or one that is not favourable, they are very apt to blame the letter-writer. One day a man came to me, who had often seen me writing, and asked if I would write him a few lines in answer to an advertisement. Seeing that he brought a stamped envelope and a sheet of writing-paper, and I already had pen and ink before me, I did so at once, to my sorrow. The poor fellow received no answer at all, and he was under the impression that I could so word a letter that it was certain to be successful. It never occurred to him that the advertisement being in a leading paper would be answered by hundreds of men. When several days passed, and no answer came, no doubt he came to the conclusion that he would have been more successful himself, and that I had spoilt him of that job by my manner of writing. So he was very cold after, leaving me with one consolation—that I had not only received no benefits from him, but wanted none, whether he was successful or not.

One man, who could hardly read or write, brought me his aunt's letter to be deciphered, from whom he was getting assistance every week. I had so much difficulty in reading her letter that I told him after that his aunt's writing was very bad. Hearing this he began to throw out hints that the fault must be with me, for his aunt had married a rich brewer, and was now a widow with seven servants. Seeing what a simple man I had to deal with, I tried to explain that the handwriting of some of the greatest people was bad, and that it was not their handwriting made them great, but the thoughts and language they used. But I saw that he could not understand my meaning, and he brought me no more of his aunt's letters.

In fact, the letters I have written to oblige others have made me more enemies than friends. The most grateful thanks I have received for doing this kindness was not from a man living in a lodging-house, but from one on the outside. I was in the lodging-house kitchen one night when "Brummy" Sam brought a married friend of his to see me. The former lost no time in explaining to me that his friend Alf had a daughter in service in the country. Now this daughter had been written to several times, by her mother, sister, and brother, but none of them could get an answer; so Alf, "Brummy" Sam explained, "wanted to know the ins and outs of her reasons." The latter, who had been drinking, confided to me with deep emotion that his friend Alf was a faithful old dog, and, "as for Alf's old woman, there wasn't a better-natured bleeding old cat in all London." Although he whispered this information, it was quite loud enough for Alf to hear, and the big fellow looked at Sam with gratitude. After saying these words Sam straightened himself and said: "I have been telling Alf about you, as how you can write, and we think you can put the letter in such a way that she will answer at once." Hearing this I was not very well pleased, for I could hardly hope to be more successful than the girl's own mother. It was most likely that there was nothing the matter at all, and that she was only waiting a convenient time to write. However, I wrote a letter to Alf's daughter, which he received with so much delight, and such a pressing invitation to drink, that it quite upset me, thinking that the letter would be no more successful than others. But I am pleased to say that she not only answered it at once, but asked her mother who had written it. Perhaps she thought it was a lawyer, and was afraid that further neglect in not reporting herself at home would lead to the police court. Alf was so grateful that his friendship became a nuisance, especially when he was drunk; and I was very glad that he only came to the house as a visitor, and did not live there altogether.

But in a very common lodging-house it is not often that a man is asked to write a letter. I used to write for one man to his mother, about once a month, and he was very thankful to me, for I would never take anything from these poor fellows. It was a dreadful task for me to write a letter of that kind, for he had nothing to say except—"Give my love and say I am all right, and remember me to Aunt Sarah." And the simple man not only expected me to fill two or three papers on this meagre information, but wanted to know if I had enough paper. This man was a consumptive, and when I wrote one letter for him he was about to go into a hospital. He asked me then if I would write a few lines to his mother if anything serious happened to him. I promised to do so, but am glad to say he was back in a few weeks, although not much better.

I shall never forget writing one letter for a man who was leading a double life. He had only just come to our lodging-house, but he was so well known to all the old lodgers that I could see that he had been there before. When this man first came under my notice, he was in the act of sewing a patch on the knee of his trousers, the latter being still on his body. I may as well say here that he made a very bad job of it, for he sewed his trousers to a pair of drawers that were underneath; which made him swear so much that night, when he undressed, that irritated lodgers, disturbed from sleep, threatened to throw him out of the window. One day I asked a lodger what this man did for a living, thinking that he was either a toy-seller, paper-man, or market porter. The lodger began to chuckle, and said: "If you are down Brixton way to-morrow, you are likely to see him." As I asked the question for the sake of being sociable, and not from curiosity, I thought no more of the matter. However, some time after this I happened to be in Brixton, and saw the man I mention, standing in the gutter—blind. He saw me too, for he made an awful expression, which I translated into these words—Don't stop and speak to me, pass on. A few days after this unexpected meeting, he no sooner saw me entering the lodging-house kitchen than he came forward with an envelope and a sheet of writing paper. "Will you write me a letter?" he asked. "I will pay you." Now, I had been out all day and was hungry, and was just about to prepare my tea. So I told him sharply that if I wrote the letter I wanted nothing for doing it, and, whether I wrote it or not, he must give me a chance to have my tea first. Nearly all men that live in common lodging-houses talk to each other in this strain, for they are all more or less short-tempered, or, as they say—"scatty." So I knew that he would not take offence, and was not surprised to see him come forward, after he had given me ample time for tea. "I am not much of a scholar," he began. "What do you want me to write about?" I asked. "Well," said he, "a gentleman saw me in the street and took my address, and has just sent me a parcel of clothes, and I want to thank him. Here is his letter, with address, which was in the parcel." "All right," I answered, and did so at once. After I had done, I read aloud what I had written, and asked if it would do. He considered for a moment, and then said: "Perhaps you will write a little more and say as how Heaven will reward him for pitying a blind man." I could not help laughing at this, for he spoke so exactly that I believe the rogue had forgotten that he was not really blind.

It is very pathetic on a Christmas morning to see seventy or eighty men in a lodging-house, and not six of them receive any greetings from the outside world. In one house, where the manager's charming little daughter received scores of letters and presents from school-friends and friends of her parents, there were not ten out of ninety lodgers who received a single letter—on a Christmas morning! It was when I saw this that it came on me in full force to know what an isolated plague spot a common lodging-house is. Men who have spent years in such places must feel deeply the loneliness of their lives at that season, when every person outside a lodging-house finds time to either visit friends and relatives, or write to them.

Chapter XXVII

Licensed Beggars

With all the tricks and dodges of beggars, the man that owns a pedlar's certificate—which is known as "a brief"—is, taking it all the year round, the most successful. It matters not to him whether the police in a town are strict or not, and he is little interested when he hears street-singers or downright beggars approve or disapprove of the police in certain towns. Armed with this authority, he is a man of cool courage and impudence, and, when he produces his "brief," he makes the inquisitive constable that interferes with him, flush painfully. "Is that all the stock you have?" asks the constable sternly, glancing at the man's paltry few laces, and knowing well that he is using them for begging purposes—"Is that all the stock you carry?" "It is all I need," the other often answers impudently, shaking his laces in one hand, and his certificate in the other. All towns are not favourable to the street-singer, even though they may be good for the more silent beggar; and the downright beggar is apt at any moment to have the door answered by a policeman, and where is he then? But the licensed beggar is safe.

Now it is often very difficult to get this pedlar's certificate, although the man has the five shillings to buy it; especially in London, where a man has to be a resident in one place for six months, and must also give reasons for his request, that he is physically unfit to follow his trade or to do rough labour. But beggars know of small towns in the provinces where they only have to show five shillings and tell a lie or two, and the certificate is theirs at once. And when a man has one, the difficulty is over for all time, for he can get it renewed at the most particular town, without trouble or question.

A man may pursue his calling for a very long time without being asked to show his license, and another man may be asked to show his several times in one month, perhaps twice in one day. I knew one man that went all through the year without interference, but the very first week that his license expired and he had not renewed it, he was accosted by a policeman and arrested. This luckily turned out to his advantage, for when he explained to the magistrate his inability to save five shillings for its renewal, that gentleman generously gave him the amount out of the poor-box, and the license was renewed. Of course the man had begged enough during the week to be independent of this aid, for one lady had given him two shillings towards that end, and from several others he had received small silver instead of pennies to enable him—as he told them—"to earn an honest livelihood by selling laces, instead of begging." Yes, many a dear lady highly commended this fine, fat fellow for such a noble resolution. As I have said, he had received more than twice five shillings in the week by showing ladies his expired license, but a terrible thirst was on him, and he could not possibly pass a public-house.

It will, no doubt, be interesting news to the police, and even a number of beggars, to know that men often hide their licenses in the lining of their clothes, taking out a few stitches, and sewing up again. Quite a number of beggars sew up their valuables in their clothes, as a safeguard against loss; but the licensed beggar has another motive for doing so. The reason why he hides his license is that when he exhausts his very small stock, in an hour or two, he then takes to downright begging for the rest of the day, as he does not wish to waste time; and there may not be a swag-shop (a shop where hawkers are supplied), near, or there may not be one in the town. Now if he is arrested for begging, he will get ten days' imprisonment and, if a pedlar's license is found on him, he will receive the extra punishment of having it taken from him, and not returned. So he serves his ten days, happy to think that his "brief" is safe in the lining of his clothes. He can safely rely on this being so, for a common beggar is never subjected to a severe search.

I knew one man that had a wife and three very small children, and, on the day I made their acquaintance, she and the children remained in the lodging-house all day, so that she could do some washing. When the husband went out that morning, rather late, all his stock-in-trade consisted of was six pairs of cheap mohair laces, which cost him threepence, and with these he went to work. Soon he returned with one shilling and ninepence in coppers, four parcels of food, and two pairs of laces still left. Eighteen pence had to be paid for their night's lodging, without a question of food for five bodies. Giving his wife the money, he again sailed forth for the afternoon. In four hours he returned with one and eleven pence, and no laces. After which she, having finished her washing, went out shopping, and soon returned with bread, tea, sugar, milk, mutton chops, and a fresh stock of laces; also two separate half-ounces of tobacco, one for him and one for herself. With this supply, and the contents of her husband's pockets—he regretted that he could not carry more—the family could do very well for tea, supper, and breakfast the next morning. This industrious couple were always very successful on Sunday mornings, when they sang hymns in the street, with the three small children at their side.

One of the most versatile beggars that I have ever met was Harry the Whistler, who was so resourceful that he was indifferent whether his wife remained idle at home in the lodging-house or not. He also carried a "brief," with a few pins and needles, for the benefit of odd houses scattered here and there; but when he saw a number of houses close together, or anything that looked like a street, he would immediately make a stand and blow a tin whistle. Sometimes, to relieve the monotony, he and his wife sang together, but more often than not she stood silently at his side, and received the reward of his playing.

The first time I met this couple, Harry the Whistler had to go to bed early, so that his wife could mend the bottom of his trousers. They almost came to blows on this occasion, for the wife maintained that she would not sit up late night after night to mend his trousers, and that if he would still persist in blowing a tin whistle, and having the bottom of his trousers torn by dogs, instead of going in for chanting, peddling, or straight begging, she would no longer travel with him. After he had cursed dogs to his heart's content, he confessed that it was no more pleasure for him to go to bed early than it was for her to sit up late and mend his trousers, and that in the future he would cease playing as soon as his notes were answered by a dog's bark.

Chapter XXVIII

Navvies and Frauds

Navvies in common lodging-houses receive much contempt from pedlars, grinders, and true beggars. They are always washing clothes and making shackles (soup) on Sunday, owing to their perspiration and dry food during the week; and while they are going about these long tasks, others cannot find accommodation. They always manage to get the use of the whole fire—centre, sides, and front—just before public-houses open; after which they booze until closing time, and then return to fill every utensil in the kitchen—basins, teacups, and saucers—with their greasy shackles. Although generous to one another, they would not let the smell of their shackles reach true beggars, if it could be prevented; and yet, when a navvy is reduced to the price of his bed only, he hints at his wants in a common lodging-house kitchen, expecting assistance from beggars, instead of making his wants known outside.

The navvy is more often than not a very timid beggar, and, when he can, lives upon stolen apples, turnips, blackberries, etc.; aye, and the picked-up bread that true beggars have cast away. In spite of this, I have seen an exceptional navvy that had the impudence to stand pad in a crowded market-place; which means that he would stand in the street gutter with a few laces or pins in his hand, a thing that only afflicted ones are expected to do. He does this on the night that follows pay-day, and it must be confessed that he meets with some reward. Sometimes a servant girl gives him a penny through admiration of his stalwart form; sometimes an old lady gives him a penny because his nose is like her son's; and, seeing that on this particular night everybody is happy with money in their pockets, it is not to be surprised at that a number of stray coppers find their way into his pocket. In this instance, charity is certainly not misplaced, for this man would rather work than beg. If he was engaged to be at your house to do a job on the following day, you could have little doubt but what he would appear. Only one thing would prevent him, and that is the arrival at the lodging-house of moneyed navvies that have just finished a job. In that case he would not need the little work offered to him, and it would be the best policy not to absent himself from his new friends—not even for a few minutes, for, when men are drinking, they are apt to change suddenly. As long as he is face to face with them, all goes well, but he no sooner turns his back than a word of suspicion is dropped, and he returns to find that his former friends are—if not drunk—cold and reserved; and if they are drunk he will find them not only ready to quarrel, but to murder.

The navvy is a real working-man, but he has to travel for work from place to place, and his jobs are very often short through no fault of his own. Being a rough, uncouth, and ill-mannered man, fond of drink and freedom to chew and smoke tobacco, to spit, and use strong language, he has no other option than to live in a common lodging-house, even though he is earning as much money as a good mechanic.

Now, although a navvy spends the best part of his life among beggars in common lodging-houses, it is surprising how simple and innocent he is as to beggars' tricks and dodges. If he saw a man in a fit in the street, the navvy would be one of the last to suspect that man of being a fraud. If he saw a man making feeble attempts to climb a bridge's wall or railings, and drop into the river, the navvy would be the last to have suspicion that that man was doing so to introduce himself to one who would listen to his pitiful story, and help him with a shilling or more. And the navvy would never suspect the child that pretends to lose money and begins to cry in a loud voice. And yet this navvy spends his life in a lodging-house, where these cunning mortals live.

These tricks are not so common as people suppose; they are in fact very rare. Many an honest man has fits, the rivers give up a number of suicides, and with regard to the child losing money—was there ever a child that did not?

Beggars have various ways by which they can get shillings instead of pennies. When a beggar in a lodging-house kitchen produced a massive ring for the inspection of his fellow lodgers, it was eagerly commented on as "a good one"; by which they meant to say that it was a good imitation, for they all knew that it was a dummy. But a navvy saw that it was marked so many carats, felt that it was heavy, saw that it was of good colour, and exclaimed, to the derision of the lodgers assembled: "It's real gold! Did you pick it up?" "Will you give me sixpence for it?" asked the other. The navvy did not answer, for this question seemed to enlighten him.

The ring dodge is a paying concern, for the sale of one ring often means dinner, drinks, supper, bed, and breakfast. The ring is, to all appearance, valuable; according to its colour, finish, weight, and—the best sign of all—its mark of carats. All that is to be done is to invite inspection, and if you are suspected of being a thief who is afraid to enter a pawnshop, so much the better, for you are almost certain to find an avaricious victim. Very few men can resist giving a couple of shillings for an article which they feel satisfied can be again easily disposed of at a good profit. I have often been invited as a would-be purchaser to examine a ring in the hand of a seedy-looking man, and, if he persists, I simply say, "I live in a doss-house," and he does not waste any more time on me.

Then there is the razor-man, with his very cheap razors, which look so very good. It is generally in public-houses where the razor-man succeeds. Producing a fine-looking razor, he invites inspection, and when it meets with approval he offers it for sale. If he cannot get more than three times its worth, he is in bad luck indeed.

Then there is the man who carries a few cheap spectacles, which never cost him more than twopence-halfpenny a pair. At night this man finds victims in public-houses, and by day the ladies must suffer. Sometimes he carries a few laces, pins, and needles, etc., so as to get a few coppers at places where spectacles would not be needed. When an elderly lady answers the door, he, after a while, introduces the spectacles, taking them from his inside pocket. It is more than probable that she uses glasses to read and sew, even if she is not wearing them then.

In a case of this kind women, also men, are very curious, and they cannot resist the temptation to try the glasses, even though they are well suited with what they possess. Moreover, it is well to have several pairs of glasses, in case of accidents.

Now, sometimes a very common pair of glasses will suit better than costly ones for which the eyes were tested; even as a brass watch may keep better time than a gold one, or a pair of ready-made boots fit better than a pair made to order. If the old lady is satisfied that she can see as well as with her own, the glasses at once assume value, and this is known to the pedlar, for he never mentions a word about price until he hears her verdict. First she tries one pair, and then another, until she confesses that one pair in particular suits her eyes. On hearing this the man gives his price, which is according to what he thinks the woman can afford. If she can afford to make a purchase, she does, and tells him that she can see better with his eighteen-penny glasses than with a pair for which her eyes were tested, and which cost her seven shillings and sixpence, or more. And these spectacles cost the pedlar two shillings and sixpence per dozen.

A little originality converts a common beggar into a great one. When I was in the Welsh hills, where common lodging-houses were scarce, I found a house to my liking, and, seeing that there were a number of good-sized towns near, within three or four miles, determined to make it my quarters for a month or more, and thoroughly work the country around. I was selling laces at the time, and on my visit to one of the towns, I had remarkably good luck. Seeing a long street, I called at every house and received in all one shilling and twopence for my trouble, with the sale of four pairs of laces, which cost me less than twopence. I mentioned this to a fellow-lodger, who had been staying at the house for several days. When at his request I described the position of the street, he said, with a quiet smile: "I got eight shillings and sixpence out of that street." "What were you selling?" I asked, thinking he must be in a large way of business, and wondering why he lived at a common lodging-house. "Nothing," he answered, to my amazement; "it was all profit." This made me curious, for I knew that he, being a man apparently unafflicted and in good health, could not be very successful as a plain beggar. Before we went to bed this man gave me a letter to read, and in this letter it said that he was one of the strikers at M—, and that he had a wife and four children to maintain, and ended with a polite and dignified request for assistance. With this letter he did his business, simply handing it to whoever answered the door, with the request that they would take it in and read it. His time was night, when the whole family were at home, probably two or three working sons and the father; and when he could go from door to door without attracting notice.

Who could insult this man with a common penny? No doubt two or three people that had given me pennies refused this more ambitious man; but others, who thought a penny quite enough for me, gave him sixpence or a shilling. The letter—what originality! It did not give a servant chance to dismiss him, for she had no suspicion of his wants; and it did not give one of the family power to speak for all. And yet, in spite of knowing these tricks, I still continued the far less profitable traffic in laces.

Chapter XXIX

A First Night in a Lodging-house

I have lived so full a life that I forgot, till lately, an incident that other men would, if it was their experience, talk about till the end of their days; for it was at that time that I first became acquainted with common lodging-houses and shelters. It was when I was young, twenty years of age, and had just finished my apprenticeship, that I paid my fare to London, and then had five weeks' experience of the worst side of life. When I arrived in London, I had a gold sovereign and a few shillings; and, being full of hope, like all young people, went to a small hotel, had a good meal, and paid two shillings and sixpence for my bed. At this rate I was soon bankrupt, and then commenced my experience of real life; for I was soon hungry and walking the streets at night. But on the first night I had the good fortune to be assisted by a gentleman who, seeing me standing under an arch, asked a few questions and then gave me sixpence. This was my first experience of acute hunger, and it so frightened me that when day came, and I had had a cup of tea and a slice of bread and butter, I bought half a pennyworth of stationery and a stamp and sent home for money, having the reply addressed to a post office in the Strand. The following day I received a letter with a postal order for twenty shillings. A few days had taught me much, and I was now determined to spend no more half-crowns on beds, but to make this money last as long as possible. So I asked a ragged man what was the cheapest bed I could get, and he said fourpence, but that I could get a bunk at the Salvation Army shelter for twopence. Leaving him I went in quest of a fourpenny lodging-house in the East End, and soon found one. That was my first experience in a common lodging-house, but I cannot say that at that time the experience filled me with anything like horror. I was young and romantic, and felt proud in having such a strange experience, which I could talk about when I would be in a better position, to people's amazement. However, I only stayed there three nights, because I saw that I would soon be hungry again, if I did not seek cheaper lodgings. So I made enquiries about a Salvation Army shelter, and was soon inside one in Ratcliff Highway. I did not think this place quite so romantic as the common lodging-house, for here were so many men that not one could be seated with comfort, and these men were more ragged and dirtier.

Now, at this time I was a pure-minded youth, who had been a chapel-goer, by compulsion 'tis true; and I thought the world was divided into two classes—the wicked, who never went to a place of worship, and the good, who went every Sunday at least. I had never given it a thought what a hypocrite was, and that people would go to church or chapel from other motives than religion. For this reason what surprised and shocked me most at this shelter was to hear the Salvation Army soldiers using bad language. I could hardly believe my ears, when I heard them, even on Sunday, before and after a meeting in which they had prayed and sung.

The bunks in this shelter were on the floor, and contained a mattress covered with leather, and a leather quilt. This was quite sufficient for warmth, for every man lay in his clothes, and so many men together made the air warm and very foul. Each bunk was about six feet long, two feet and a half wide, and six inches in height. I need hardly say that I soon got homesick; and when I heard a couple of sailors say that they were going to South Wales to look for a ship, I at once offered to accompany them. Luckily for me these two sailors were good cadgers, having often tramped across country to different seaports, so that I was not likely to starve in their company. The next morning, when I told them I had a silver shilling left, and took their advice to spend it on ale and tobacco, they promised with many oaths that I should not want for food on the road. But I only accompanied them a little more than half-way, and then left them; for they, having no sure prospects, were not inclined to tax their walking strength to the utmost. My last stage was over sixty miles, with only one stop, and that was nine miles from home. It was then night, and I met a policeman who wanted to know where I was going. "Home," I answered, and added the name of the town. I began to feel a bit tired now, and sat on a bank for a few moments' rest, after which I rose and continued my way. But I had hardly gone twenty yards when I met a policeman again, who said: "Hallo! what are you doing here? I thought you were going home?" "So I am," I answered, quite bewildered. "You are going away from it," he said; "you have walked back two miles from where I met you before." When I had sat on the bank I must have fallen asleep, and, waking, did not know in the dark but what I was going right. However, at that time these experiences only made romance. The truth is that as long as the young do not feel actual hunger, they care little for other things. And I was very fortunate in these few weeks, for I was never forced to beg. The two sailors not only fed me, but, when I left them, gave me as much food as I was likely to want on my way home. It was years after, when I began to feel literary ambition and wanted privacy, that I experienced the horror of being mixed with thirty or forty men in a small lodging-house kitchen.

One day, when I had been in a common lodging-house for a considerable time, I met a man in Hyde Park, who had lately come from the country, and was now come to his last shilling, after selling whatever he had of value. Hearing this, I could do no other than take him to the lodging-house where I lived. I gathered from his conversation that he had no idea of such places. Now it happened that I was living in a very low-class house in Blackfriars, whose inmates were not only very poor and ragged, but rough and brutal; so, when I began to think of this, I almost repented of my offer to take charge of him. However, it was too late now, so on we went, and were soon at the house. When we entered the kitchen there were three of the worst lodgers quarrelling, and not only drunk, but with a can full of beer on the table. What must have been this man's thoughts, who had only just left a good home? for he had been telling me about his mother and sisters. I told him to sit down and wait until I returned from shopping, after which we would have tea. I was away less than ten minutes, for there were several shops near, but when I came back he had gone. Speaking to one of the lodgers about him, I was told that he had followed me out, close at my heels. I never saw him again. I believe that he was so disgusted with his strange surroundings that he started for home at once, although it was a hundred miles away. His feelings must have been very strong, seeing that he had already paid for his bed, and that sum was now lost to him. I have often wondered what must have been his final opinion of me, to whom he had entrusted his confidence. Perhaps he thought that I had decoyed him there to be robbed of his very clothes. The place must have seemed horrible to him, with its dark, underground kitchen, no woman there, and nothing, except a cat, to make it appear like a home.

Of course, I am speaking now of the very lowest lodging-houses—houses that are seldom written about; for journalists choose better-class lodging-houses for their visits. Some time ago, I read an account of a journalist going to spend one night in a lodging-house. He explained how he pocketed his briar pipe, and took a common clay one, and how he dirtied his face and hands. Now it happened that the house he went to was a superior lodging-house where he would see a number of men with silk hats and watches and chains. In fact, this innocent journalist made himself ill-looking enough for a fourpenny lodging-house, and I would not have been surprised if he had been refused a bed at the house to which he went. After reading his account I have come to the conclusion that he did not visit the place at all.

Speaking of journalistic work, I know a book that describes low life in London, with pictures taken from life. When I look at one picture I see a man and a woman with a handcart loaded with household furniture. These two are leaving a house at night, for they owe rent. But when I look closer still, I recognize both the man and the woman; and I know that the former has been in a lodging-house for twenty years, during which time he never had furniture. I also know that the woman has not for thirty years had cause to do what the picture represents. Of course, this does not matter, for such things are to be seen—but the picture was not taken from real life. The picture was taken by day, when people do not make "moonlight flits"; and at night—which the scene represents—the great journalist was sleeping in his luxurious home.

Chapter XXX

Gentleman Bill

A man may not only play many parts in life, but sometimes even his real character undergoes a change and conforms to his surroundings. Such was the case with Gentleman Bill. When he first came to our lodging-house he was a quiet, modest man, who was almost too timid to hazard a suggestion on the most common subjects; but in less than three months conceit and importance was so thrust upon him that he was almost too proud to walk. I was a witness of this development of a new character, right from the beginning, and saw that Bill was not in any way to blame; but that the ignorance of his associates shoved him, in spite of his modesty, shoulder-high above themselves. Bill, it appeared to me, had mixed, ere his downfall, with people who were his equal, and not a few of whom were his superior—hence his modesty when he first came to our house as a needy lodger.

He was seen to be a very quiet man, always reading newspapers or books, or walking silently up and down the kitchen in deep thought. For a month or more the lodgers took very little notice of him, but when his appearance had grown familiar to them, they began to ask his opinion on different subjects— cooking, physic, the nutritious value of foods, the meaning of words, the use of the House of Lords, and many other interesting things. These questions were answered by Bill in such a high-flown manner, as became a great reader, that really his hearers were little the wiser, and came to the conclusion that Bill's knowledge was far too deep for them. The lodgers were so awestruck at Bill's easy delivery of unusual words that they could not grasp the underlying thought. It was not long before he became so puffed with his own importance, and so eager to express his opinions, that he did not wait an invitation to join in a conversation, but stood in the middle of the kitchen and spoke in such a masterly way that some of the lodgers thought that he was an ex-M.P. He was not satisfied with giving his own opinions, but quoted poets, philosophers, lawyers, and statesmen; and the lodgers at last became so impressed that they sought him all over the house to hear him settle an argument. One morning Little Brum actually took a cup of tea to Gentleman Bill, while the latter was in bed, so as to get him down to settle a dispute which was likely to make the principals lose a morning's work.

It was not long before Bill had to pay the penalty of being so important, for some of the more simple lodgers began to ask him such idiotic questions that Bill, who up to the present had never been at a loss for a word, could do little more than stand dumb with amazement. For instance, one day a poor simple fellow asked the following question: "Is it right to post a letter to-day that was written yesterday?" An Irishman asked him the belief of the laity, and whether they were for or against the Pope of Rome. Another had heard that an egg boiled too hard could be again boiled soft, and wanted to know if it could be boiled to recover its first raw state. Poor Bill began to lose patience and grumble, saying that he could not be expected to know everything. The lodgers would not allow him peace to have a cup of tea, to shave, wash, or read.

I happened to be sleeping in the same room as Bill, a large room with seven beds to accommodate seven men. Early one morning, about three o'clock, I was in that half-wakeful state when a man turns his body over in sleep, and thought I heard voices. Curiosity getting the better of sleep, I listened, and sure enough the man in the next bed to Bill was asking him a number of questions. The questions must have interested Bill, for he immediately sat up in bed and began a long talk. When I fell asleep he was still sitting up and talking, and I did not wonder that he was a late riser.

On one occasion there was a terrible fuss in the house, and a lodger called Bill a damned conspirator. It seemed that the man had claimed a letter at the office which did not belong to him. When the clerk received letters he wrote the surnames on a sheet of paper, which he placed in the window. The Christian names were kept secret, so that he could question applicants about them, this being the only plan of placing letters in the right hands. Where there were such a number of men there were certain to be several of the name of Smith, Jones, Brown, and other common names. So when one morning the clerk received a letter for William Henry, he added the surname to his list. Reading the list of names a simple lodger, whose Christian name was Henry, made application for the said letter. The clerk got the letter and, glancing at the envelope, made his usual enquiry, "Your Christian name?" Now it happened that the man did not know the meaning of this question, and to be on the safe side he gave his full name, which was Henry Brown. The clerk lost patience at Brown's simplicity and said, "This letter is not for you; your Christian name is Henry, but the man to whom this letter belongs is surnamed Henry." The dissatisfied and unconvinced lodger left the office and sought Gentleman Bill, whom he found and consulted. Bill went into a long discourse as to the origin of surnames, but the lodger cut him short by asking what right the clerk had to place his name on the list and not give up the letter. It was no use for Bill to try to explain the difference between surnames and Christian names, and he was no more successful than the clerk, although he took fifty times the time and words. The upshot of it was that the infuriated lodger called Bill a damned conspirator, whereas Bill also lost his calmness and called the lodger a fool.

How Bill was spoilt by so much consultation was made apparent to me by a little incident that escaped the notice of others. He had been having a glass or two of ale, and, coming into the kitchen with his book, which was a grammar, seated himself comfortably at the fire. The effect of the ale, the heat of the fire, and the inactive state of his body, soon made Bill bow his head to the table, and in a minute or two he was fast asleep. I happened to be sitting near him at the time, and was taken by surprise to hear his voice. Thinking he was addressing me I turned, but saw that he was fast asleep and talking to himself. All at once I heard him say, as distinctly as though he had been awake, "What I need is a silk hat and a frock-coat"; meaning, of course, that if he had those things, for the sake of appearance, his knowledge, conversation, and manners would be the making of him.

On one or two occasions I had the honour of being consulted by Bill—of which I am very proud, for he did not consider any other man in the house able to teach him anything. I had always managed to satisfy him with my remarks, but when he approached me one night, with his grammar book in his hand, and asked me if I knew anything about the infinitive split, the question almost took my breath away.

Certainly I had heard of it, heard enough to know that it was to be avoided as a subject of argument, or it would soon worry a man to a shadow. I told Bill at once that I could not enlighten him, and advised him not to worry over it. This advice was not taken, for he bought two more cheap second-hand grammar books, and still could not get on the track of the infinitive split. In less than three weeks his voice was low and weak, his face became haggard and thin, his hair lay uncombed on his forehead, and his bones began to show their shape under the skin. He was not even civil in those days, and no longer felt the importance of being consulted. He requested the lodgers not to bother him, that he had other things on his mind, and far more trouble than he could contend with.

Yes. Bill was a nice fellow when he first came to the house, modest and unassuming; he was also interesting to hear when he became confident and assertive; but after he fell foul of the infinitive split, he became a man to be avoided, and his curt answers made many a man frown.

Chapter XXXI

Fallacies Concerning Beggars

There are quite a number of fallacies, concerning beggars, which are sadly in need of contradiction, so that these much-misunderstood men may stand in their innocence before the public. They do not mark houses, as is commonly supposed; they do not spend the money of charity on drink; they do not possess hidden hoards; and they have as much dread of meeting women in lonely places as the latter have of meeting them.

In the first place, why should they mark houses? If you enter a common lodging-house in the country, you will find, on making enquiry, that two out of three beggars have been there before, and know from past experience one or more good houses; but they would rather share their spoils with you than show these houses, or explain their where-abouts. Beggars, however good-natured they may be in a lodging-house, are all selfish on this one point. They always live in expectation of future benefits from those houses, and it is not likely that they will risk spoiling them by giving information to others who may not approach them in a proper manner, or may even be impudent. If you ever see a house marked you may be sure that it is by one of a family, who are working different parts of the town, and who will change about on the following days. Private people seem to know more of this matter than beggars, for, after visiting more than a hundred lodging-houses, and hearing the conversation of thousands of beggars, I have not heard one whisper of a marked house.

Another belief is that beggars possess secret hoards. Because people in years of reading have seen two or three accounts of cases of this kind, they are under the impression that half the beggars that approach them are misers that would rather beg than buy. Now good beggars will still work on the public feeling with three or four shillings' worth of coppers in their pockets, but you could search the first thousand you met and be very unlikely to find gold. The most persistent beggars will often beg hard until they have saved a few shillings, after which they feel justified in taking a much-deserved rest, and are often to be seen idling for a couple of days in a town that is no good for begging, but where the accommodation of the lodging-house is excellent.

Another fallacy is that they are eager to molest women and children. It is a mystery how these charges can be made against them, for few cases of the kind get into the papers. The only way to account for this belief is that all undiscovered violence and petty crime is put down to be the work of tramps, and the papers are only too eager to take such a view. When a man fell from his bicycle, trying to avoid running over an old deaf tramp, the local press thought it would make better copy to say that the man was knocked off his bicycle by a vicious tramp, much to the surprise of the man himself.

Again, a tramp does not like to meet a woman in a lonely place, and he often whistles loudly so as to encourage her not to faint, and he never forgets to give her plenty of room to pass, and nothing annoys him more than to see timid children run into their houses at his approach. A tramp likes to have women answer the door to him, when they have the confidence of being surrounded by neighbours; but when it comes to the open air, women are a nuisance to him, and he would be glad if no women walked abroad. He can approach his own sex and speak, but he is afraid of being within ten feet of a woman's nerves.

Then there is the fallacy that he is spending money on drink, because he is seen going in or out of a public-house. People do not know that he enters as a beggar, not as a customer, and that he often gets tipsy because beer is often easier to beg than bread or pennies. I have seen hundreds of beggars drunk who had not spent one penny on drink. On a Saturday night, almost every man in a common lodging-house is drunk, and often against his wish. All beggars know that they can do almost as well on a Saturday night by telling their tales in public-houses, as they can by calling at private houses all through the week; and in doing so they get drunk on free drinks, without having spent one of the many pennies they have received from customers.

Another fallacy is that beggars are the authors of so many deeds of barn-burning, theft, and assaults on women who could not recognize their assailants in the dark. It is quite a common thing to hear tramps in a common lodging-house say, "Tramps, of course, will be blamed for this," when one of them reads aloud of an undiscovered crime. Sometimes the real culprits are at last found, and though they are not strange tramps, but people of the locality, yet no one thinks of apologizing for the unjust suspicion on tramps.

They do not often burn hayricks for spite, as is commonly supposed. They may accidentally burn one through smoking. It should be understood that they are very careful not to do so, or they would have to walk until they were miles away, and would rob themselves of a comfortable night's rest. No, farmers have jealous neighbours and discontented labourers, who are worse enemies than strange tramps. Idle threats, due to irritation, are generally the extent of their crime. Is it likely that a beggar who has been refused food at a house will hide somewhere and nurse vengeance for hours, so that he may break into it or set fire to it at night? He is hungry, and he must travel on in search of food, and he will at last meet with success; and there is not a man in the world more innocent of acts of crime than he is then, when his empty body is satisfied. He forgets all past unkindness, and the household that he has threatened to murder has passed out of his recollection for ever.

People should know that tramps talk aloud to themselves, owing to being so much alone. Therefore, when a woman refuses a tramp on the score of a husband doing little work, and the said tramp goes away muttering, she must not at once come to the conclusion, as she always does, that he is cursing her; for it is more than likely that he is cursing some cause he imagines has placed her in such a helpless position.

There is one thing against a beggar that has been witnessed so often that it would be folly to dispute the truth of it, which is that he throws food away. Although he cannot be altogether justified, yet an explanation of the real facts may go far to make people sympathize with his dilemmas.

People seldom take into consideration that he needs a bed, and they would often rather give him two-penny-worth of food than a halfpenny in money. Now a beggar knows that if he asks at a house point-blank for money, nothing will he get; or, occasionally a woman will say, "I will give you something to eat." For that reason he always asks for food, and then gets an odd penny here and there—which he would not get if he asked for money. But it is often necessary to beg so much food in getting a few coppers for his lodging and a little tea and tobacco, that he soon gets encumbered with more food than he can hide or eat. In this case he cannot continue begging—which he must, or go into the workhouse—so he throws the food away and continues to beg more of it, in the hope of getting money for his bed. But very few beggars ever threw food away without feeling regret that they had to do so. It is for this reason that so many beggars carry a few cheap trifles, such as pins, needles, laces, or some self-made novelty. With these things they are sure of getting money for their lodging, and, while doing so, beg food from those that will not buy.

I hope by these explanations to have made a beggar worthy of kinder consideration, and proved his to be a character to be loved and respected. Henceforth let no lady be afraid to walk a lonely road without a dog, for her presence is dreaded by a tramp, however beautiful she may be. The tramp has not Tommy Atkins's eye for female beauty.

Let no total abstainer, who has given a beggar a penny, and sees him enter a public-house, think that the penny goes for beer, for a beggar is more likely to go in to beg instead of buy.

Think not because you have read of one case where a beggar was arrested and found to have considerable money sewn in his clothes, that every beggar you meet has saved money.

Think not because a beggar was seen in the morning to pass a barn that was burned to the ground that same night, that he was the guilty one. A burning barn would not feed his body, and he would not remain there long enough to warm his feet and dry his socks.

And if you still believe that beggars mark houses, go to the window and watch every one that leaves, and you are likely to be a great many years before you catch one in the act of doing so. Houses are marked, but in nine cases out of ten children are the guilty ones.

Chapter XXXII

Lady Tramps

Almost all tramps who travel alone object to women in a common lodging-house. Even the landlord of such a place soon learns from experience that women take out in accommodation the worth of their money, for they make the place too much of a home. If they are bad wives they are continually squabbling with their husbands, or scolding their children; if they are good wives they are always cooking, or covering the limited number of seats and tables with sewing material, or surrounding the fire with newly washed clothes; and the poor bachelor, who is more indifferent to cleanliness, and often prefers a slice of bacon quickly done to the labour of cooking vegetable meals—this poor bachelor complains not only that he cannot get near the fire, but that there is not enough room on the tables to lay his food, which is not often the truth.

As for the landlords, they are becoming more bitter every day, and these unfortunate women now find it so difficult to get lodgings, that they dare not visit any town haphazard, but must make enquiries of their fellow travellers as to accommodation for women. Often they hear, to their disappointment, of houses that formerly lodged women being changed into houses for men only. And if these women have children, matters are still worse, for they are objected to on that account. It is therefore not the least wonder that when a man, his wife, and two or more children, succeed in being lodged, they are loth to leave that town until they have tapped it thoroughly—north, south, east, and west, house and shop; and sometimes they remain so long in that one town—perhaps three months or more—that their faces become known, and they are not supposed to belong to a tribe of wanderers. It is in the summer months, when the nights are warm, and they are independent of lodging-houses, that they prove themselves to be true travellers.

Perhaps it is because women are so much better beggars than men that they are disliked both by bachelor beggars and lodging-house keepers. The former know well that if a woman once starts in a street, she will carry all before her—money, clothes, and food; and the landlords know that a woman is so successful that she is soon back again in the lodging-house; in fact she is often there twenty-three hours out of the twenty-four. Whereas the man, however good a beggar he may be, is absent several hours in a day, for he not only takes much longer than a woman to earn a living, but he is fond of standing at street corners, and sometimes he visits a library. The woman is instinctively inclined to make the place a home, but the man more often uses it simply as a place wherein to eat and sleep.

The woman, whether she has little ones or not, is always believed when she claims to have a family, and she receives wearing apparel for them, and food. The former she sells cheaply to the poor but more respectable class of people that live in the locality of cheap lodging-houses. But the man can never do business with children in the spirit; he needs them in the flesh at his side, or he is not believed to be a father.

After a woman has been on the road a little time and become familiar with lodging-houses and begging, she finds little difficulty in maintaining a husband that will neither work, beg, nor steal—especially if she has a child for the poor fellow to look after; to wheel in a box, when he must take great care to stop in front of the house where his wife is. The most hard-hearted cannot withhold their charity, for the child's sake. As soon as the man hears the front door open, he must become very interested in his offspring, and move in a circle round the box, trying to make the child more comfortable. His solicitude is almost certain of reward, for the lady of the house cannot fail to see this, and her tender heart overflows in pity for the whole family. "Whatever his faults are," thinks she, "he undoubtedly has a father's feeling for the poor child." Of course the father is as fond of his child as any other father would be, and he would do anything in reason for it—anything, except work.

Another objection lodging-house keepers have to women lodgers is that when they begin a quarrel they are so long in bringing it to an end, especially if under the influence of drink. Whereas in the case of men it is often a short violent tussle of two or three minutes—fifteen minutes would be unusual for two untrained men—and that is the end of it, for neither one has a wish to renew hostilities. It is all over before a constable can be found, much less dragged unwillingly to the battle ground.

"Yes," I heard one lady lodger say to a landlord, who had threatened to eject her for speaking her mind—"Yes," said she, "and if I had Liverpool Nora and Brummagem Sal at my side, instead of this"—pointing to her husband—"we would soon see who's who in a very short time." Some time after I had the pleasure of meeting Liverpool Nora, and my opinion is that if Brummagem Sal was as high-spirited and brawny as that lady, well, it would be folly to aggravate them singly, much less the twain.

There is one man who favours the presence of women, and that is the true working-man, who is travelling for work, and after paying his last few coppers for a bed, sits hungry in the lodging-house kitchen, for he is a poor beggar indeed. As a rule the men are indifferent, but these women always guess his secret and pity him. They watch, and if they see no sign of food cooked, or to be cooked, it is not long before he is asked to have a basin of broth or stew, and, if he accepts, the other women—being now correct in their surmises—supply him with bread. In fact, after this initial movement, he is certain of a full stomach as long as he remains at that particular house. Many a poor fellow would have gone supperless to bed, and begun another weary day's march without breakfast, were it not for some thoughtful and unselfish beggar woman in a lodging-house kitchen.

Now, as I have said, five women under the influence of drink are less likely to go quietly to bed than twenty or thirty men in the same condition, and that is the landlord's one just objection to female lodgers. With regard to his other objections they are of little account; for, though these women are in the kitchen almost the whole day, continually using the cooking utensils and the fire, do they not wash the former and keep the latter's hearth clean? If he had all male lodgers he would have to keep a man or woman to do these things, or either he or his wife be kept busy; for no lodger, whether it be man, woman, or child, can be expected to do these things themselves, after paying for accommodation. The truth of the matter is that these landlords are like a good many others—they want both rent and possession; and it is the limited number of these places—especially for families—that makes these men so independent.

Sometimes, where the accommodation is outrageously bad, the woman lodger stores her resentment until it serves her purpose, and, the morning she is going away, she will often make an hour's delay to tell the landlord her opinion of his place, and he never likes to hear the truth; whereas men come and go, and are not so particular.

On one occasion I had the pleasure of hearing Irish Molly speak her mind to a landlord who begrudged coke for the kitchen fire, making it necessary for lodgers to bring in pieces of wood, picked up in the streets. Molly, her husband, and two children, had been here for two weeks, and, having thoroughly begged the town and its surrounding districts, were to seek fresh quarters on the morrow. But Molly swore the night before that she would not leave until she told the landlord what she thought of him. At nine o'clock on the following morning, they were ready to leave, and in spite of the husband's hurry to be off, Molly would not budge until she saw the lodging-house keeper. At last that gentleman entered the kitchen, and Molly at once rose to her feet, and set on him like a fury. For a moment the man was astonished, and tried to pacify her, but failing to do so, he hurriedly left the kitchen, and took refuge in his private room. Irish Molly at once followed and, standing outside, emphasized her words with her fists on the door. For ten minutes she hammered and abused, and the men and women in the kitchen encouraged her with their laughter. "I shall send for a constable," shouted the landlord from behind the door. "Send for fifty," cried Molly. "I shall have you locked up," he shouted. "Come out, and be knocked down," cried she.

Now it happened that Molly's husband and two children had stood waiting at the front door all this time. More than once he had asked her impatiently if she was coming, and at last, receiving no answer, went away with the children. Love in Molly's bosom was stronger than revenge, for she at once prepared to follow them. But, wishing to give the lodging-house keeper a new specimen of her powers, she sang him one verse of a ditty, beginning, "O, I am waiting for you, love." After which she danced the chorus down the wooden passage, arriving at the front door just in time to give it the final high kick.

Chapter XXXIII

Meeting Old Friends

It is a great pleasure to have a sharp eye and a clear memory for people we have met years ago, if only for a few minutes, and try to remember the condition under which they were met. For this reason I always enjoy a day in London, for I am sure to meet some strange characters that surprised or amused me in days gone by. These people do not know me. Perhaps their eyesight is not so good as mine, or their memories are not so clear. Moreover, they do not study character, and one man to them is much the same as another, with only the difference of outward appearance.

When I met a man the other day in Fleet Street, I touched him lightly on the shoulder and said, "Have a drink?" "Certainly," he answered, looking at me very hard; "but I don't remember meeting you before." After we had drunk part of our beer, I asked him if he had read anything of the scandal in high life, which the papers were then making much of. Now I had only met this man once, and that had been years before, in a common lodging-house in Blackfriars Road. On that occasion he had laid claim in fierce tones to the very purest French blood, and had laughed to scorn the blood of our English aristocracy. As soon as I mentioned this scandal in English high life, the man immediately began in his old manner to compare the blood of England to that of France, and proved to me at once that he had the same subject for his delight.

After I left him I wandered into the Embankment Gardens, and there I saw a very ragged man sleeping on a seat. I recognized him at once, in spite of a great change in appearance. He was the man whom I met at a superior lodging-house, who hid himself when a celebrated Duchess was brought there to see the place. He told me, after she had gone, that he had been valet to the Duke, but that the lady had never liked him, and had at last succeeded in getting him dismissed. At that time he looked healthy, clean, and was well dressed, but he did not want the Duchess to see him in a lodging-house. Suppose she saw him now, ragged, dirty, and without a house of any kind.

In the same house I knew many other queer characters, whom I often meet now. There was the man that starved on a small allowance made by his brother, and knew so much about finance and yet could make no money. Occasionally he received a few shillings for an article on finance, but he had hard work to keep body and soul together.

Another strange character was Darky. This man had read verses to every one of the four hundred regular lodgers at the house, and hardly one stranger that came there for a single night escaped without hearing him. Seeing that every lodger in the house knew him for a poet, I had the good sense to confide in no one; for I knew that the dignity of a poet had suffered for all time, as far as this house was concerned. Darky had written an ode to the man who founded this class of lodging-house, and had received personal thanks. The Boer War kept him busy day and night, as it also did many another poet, but poor Darky could not make sixpence for one night's lodging. He had also written lines on his sister's death, which I am sorry to say he read to every stranger that would listen. He always ended by cursing his brother-in-law, that he would not—although a successful undertaker, that could have got the job done cheap—have the lines engraved on the tombstone.

I have also lately met the old-time actor, who used to borrow pennies of me, and always paid them back. One night, when I was playing a game of draughts, this old actor came and sat beside me to whisper. "I am in great difficulty," he said hurriedly; "lend me a shilling till to-morrow noon." Now a shilling was a large sum to me, and even a penny was more than I could afford to lose; for a man, however honest his intentions may be, can never be sure of paying his debts. Seeing my thoughtful expression, he said, "You shall have my watch and chain for security; I would rather let you have it than the pawnshop." A watch, thought I, is worth redeeming for a shilling, even if it is out of repair and only common metal—without a question of the chain. I did not like anyone to see our transaction, for I felt a shame in taking a security. In fact he was more careful than I was. So I slipped the shilling into his hand and received in mine something smooth, large, and round, twice the size of an ordinary watch. This manoeuvring was done with our hands under the table, but I took a swift glance downward to inspect the watch before putting it into my pocket. That it had a white face I saw at once, but what surprised me was its extraordinary lightness. However, it was not worth while to examine it more closely, for the old actor had now gone with the shilling, and I would not see him again till the morrow. When I went to bed that night I examined the watch and found it to be a most extraordinary one. It was not only common metal, but it was all in one piece, and not one part to move; and, to account for its very light weight, there was nothing inside it. I have been told since that it was a property watch, which some actors use on the stage, and was not worth twopence. This old actor was a gambler and, fortunately for me, he had a winner the next day. Knowing that honesty was the best policy—for he would soon want to borrow again—he no sooner saw me than he stepped forward with great dignity, and with a very solemn face thanked me for my kindness, paid the shilling, and received his property.

I often meet the man who has for a number of years relied on Providence for his food and lodging. On more occasions than one I have been an instrument in the hands of Providence in assisting this artful hypocrite to a meal or his bed. When in the lodging-house he is always to be seen reading the Bible, committing passages to memory, but he enters into conversation with anyone that comes near. Then he explains that although he has had no dinner, he has faith in Providence to supply his supper; and though he has no money to pay for his bed, Providence will not let him walk the streets all night. In a large house where there are more than six hundred beds, and strangers are coming and going every day, this man often finds a sympathetic ear. And in the parks and gardens, and at street corners, where he enters into conversation with strangers, he can generally get enough to keep him independent of work.

The other day I met a very small, old-fashioned looking figure dressed in black, and with a tall silk hat which looked the worse for wear. I was really startled when I saw this quaint, little, old man, for I had known him in a lodging-house five years before, and he then gave his age as ninety years. He used to sleep so sound in the chairs that lodgers believed him to be dead, and would call the manager. And when they had succeeded, after great difficulty, in rousing him, he would accuse them of trying to rob him. One day he slept so long that the porters thought that his end had come at last, and they fetched the manager. The latter did many things to rouse the old man, pinching, slapping, and shaking him, but all in vain. Giving one porter orders to send for the doctor, he told the others to carry the old man downstairs, so that the many lodgers passing to and fro would not have their attention drawn to the dead man. Taking the little figure in their strong arms, they carried it downstairs, and there it remained till the doctor came. But no sooner was that gentleman on the spot than the old man opened his eyes and, seeing to his amaze five or six men around him, scrambled to his feet and shouted, "Thieves!" The manager could not forgive this trick of the dead coming to life, and sternly bade the old man to go to his relatives, as he—the manager—had been deceived more than once.

Chapter XXXIV

The Comparison

The finest and most perfect piece of begging that was ever brought to my notice was performed in Brooklyn by Boston Shorty. Such an example in the art of begging does not deserve oblivion, so I will record it, at the same time feeling a little jealousy, which is quite natural, that I was not the hero on that occasion.

The time was morning, and Boston Shorty felt disposed for breakfast. Seeing a tenement house, with three storeys and a basement, he at once entered, and, climbing the stairway to the top storey, knocked at the door in a business-like manner—for the short one was too proud a beggar to knock humbly at any man's door. In fact, he knew well from experience that a business-like method was just as likely to meet with success as to bother his brains to invent lies. Therefore, when a stout, pleasant-looking woman answered the door, he politely wished her good morning, and with a pleased smile told her in a few words that he had come for a little breakfast—in the same manner as a landlord or his agent would ask for the rent. "Sit down," said the good woman; and Shorty at once sat down on the stairs. In a few moments she stood before him with a plate of hot buckwheat cakes and a large basin of coffee. After he had disposed of these, he again knocked at the door, and returned the empty articles, at the same time thanking the woman for her kindness. There was nothing in this act to distinguish Shorty from a thousand other beggars; but it chanced that after walking about for two or three hours, he found himself at dinner-time passing the same house. Now, no man, except a born beggar, would think of climbing the same stairs again, with so many other houses near, for in all likelihood he would be confronted by his former benefactress. But this Shorty did, for, going up to the second storey of the same tenement, he knocked at the door, which was soon answered by—the same woman! This unexpected meeting considerably surprised the short man, and it took him so long to recover his wits that the good woman, knowing his wants, came to his assistance, and called indoors, "Mrs. Smith, here's a man wants some dinner." Saying which, she smiled at Shorty and went to her own flat above.

On hearing this call, Mrs. Smith immediately came forward, and, looking at Shorty, and being satisfied with his appearance, said, "Come in."

It was after this success that Boston Shorty, when leaving the house, proved himself to be the born beggar that he was; for he at once made up his mind to consult the tenant on the main floor as to the prospects of supper. So he strayed idly about till evening, and, when supper-time came, entered the house for the third time.

Beggars have great confidence at this time of the day, for the men are at home, and kind-hearted women often refuse beggars for the simple reason that they are afraid of them. For this reason Shorty felt quite relieved when the door was answered by a man, for it was beginning to get dark, and the most kind-hearted of women are apt to be unreasonable at that time. Shorty heard a whispered consultation between the man and woman, which was soon followed by the man saying, "Walk in, my man," which the latter did.

The lady looked rather surprised when she saw Shorty's face. "Didn't I see you go upstairs at noon?" she asked. "Madam," answered the short one, not a bit abashed—"Madam, I may have done so, for the houses hereabout are so much alike."

Now, what do you think of that? Three meals in succession at one house, and from three distinct families. That in itself was a gem of begging, but to Shorty's eyes it still lacked perfection; for, during supper-time, he explained his homeless condition, and requested as another favour that they would give him an old blanket and allow him to sleep in the basement!

How it pleased my Uncle T— to hear this, who is himself a good beggar, but confines himself to Wales, with an occasional trip to an adjoining county.

Some years ago my family always referred to me as a second Uncle T—. In his young days he was a roofer, but through getting so many black eyes in taking his own part, his sight failed him so much that he could not follow his calling. It was then that he began to hawk laces, etc., and found the life to be more pleasant than hard labour. He has a strong dislike to navvies, because, I suppose, they are the hardest workers. Whenever my Uncle T— sees a gang of navvies at work, he feels while passing through them like a comet through a host of stars. It has quite upset him to hear that I have degenerated into a worker; but he is pleased to know that it is mental work, and that I never sweat or soil my hands.

It was a joy to meet him lately and hear his account of those stirring days of 1905, during the revival in Wales, when beggars had extraordinary success. His own success at that time almost ruined him, all through the generosity of a lady that had been converted. He had begged a house, and while the lady was feeding his body, she enquired with much concern about my Uncle T—'s soul. He immediately took advantage of this kind question by saying: "Lady, if there is one religious man in Wales, it is me; and yet misfortune follows me wherever I go." The upshot of this was that the lady took a house for my Uncle T—, and furnished it, and kept him for a whole month in idleness, supplying him with various sums from time to time. Then, of course, the revival burned out, and the lady began to cool towards my Uncle T—, and he began to see, to his indignation, that the lady began to suspect him of being an undeserving rogue; so he sold the furniture and took a tour through Wales. This success almost ruined him, for, after being kept so long, he found it very hard to start business again.

"America," I said to him, "is good all the year round; but it is only during revivals that this country is of much account to a beggar." "Hang the revivals," cried my Uncle T—; "for when they are over it is hard to get a crust of dry bread."

It was at this stage of the conversation that I related to him an experience of mine, which happened a few weeks before. I was in the act of washing an old shirt, not having enough money to buy a new one, and I was not rich enough to hire a washerwoman, when a knock came to the door, which I thought must be the midday post. I dried my hands, and, sure enough, it was the postman, who handed me a small dainty letter. I opened this letter at once, and the first words that caught my eyes were—"Most Distinguished Sir," and then went on to make a request for my autograph. The lady also enclosed a list of fifty or sixty names of those who had obliged her, beginning with the head of the State. That, I said to my Uncle T—, is what they call fame in England. Now let us compare it to begging in America. If I had been in that country, I could have begged a clean shirt in less time than it took to wash one, and no person there would have offered me such a ragged one.

Again, as a beggar in America I have sat down to meals consisting of turkey, sweet potatoes, mince pie, and bananas; but as a famous man in England—"I know," interrupted my Uncle T—, whose intentions had been to beg me, and whose hopes now vanished—"I know," said he, "you have to put up with anything; but why? Why don't you return to begging?" Not getting an answer to this, my Uncle T— looked considerably perplexed for the time, but at last his face brightened, and he said: "Well, lad, if you are determined on the writing business, why don't you, in the name of goodness, go in for limericks?"

Chapter XXXV

The Supper

I had been thinking all day of my strange companions of the past, both in America and England, and that accounted for my dream at night. In that dream I had invited them all to a grand supper, for I was now leading a different life. I was seated at the end of the table, which was full of fine things, and Brum, of America—the greatest beggar I had ever met—was seated at my right hand. After making them a short speech, in which I commended them on their way of living, and expressed deep regret that I had ever been cheated to follow Fame, who had led me into a treacherous swamp in which I stood up to the knees, with little power to either return or advance—after making this short speech, I invited them to help themselves, and to receive my undying friendship.

They then began to assist themselves with a hearty goodwill, all except Brum, who, to my surprise and confusion, sat motionless, glancing with scorn at his companions. "There," said he, with deep disgust; "do you call these men good beggars? See the way they rush at the food, as though they had starved themselves all day in anticipation of this meal." Saying this, he began slowly to feel the lining of his coat, and, after much trouble, took out a greasy paper parcel, placed it on his knees and began to make room for it on the table. This being done, he spread the contents before him and began to eat in a very slow and indifferent manner. As for myself, I could not eat for joy, to see all these dear faces before me, and sat smiling at one and another, laughing and sighing in turns. Sometimes I closed my eyes, and opened them again on my companions, endeared to me by a past that had few cares and worries.

By a strange coincidence, Irish Tim of London was paired with Oaklahoma Sam of America. Now the latter was a man of very few words, and he always had in hand a long dangerous-looking knife, with which he trimmed his nails, whittled sticks, or threw at cracks in the door, flies, or any other object that caught his eye. But he never allowed that knife to remain long out of his hand, for, if he threw it at a door nine feet away, he was sure to recover it at one leap, and ere it had finished trembling in the wood. When I have seen him asleep at the cattleman's office, he always had this knife between his teeth.

As I have said, Sam was a man of few words, but on the subject of war he was more talkative than an old man. His memory on that one subject was extraordinary; knowing the dates of battles, the number of their forces, names of generals and regiments, and the exact position of their entrenchments. Tim must have unwittingly broached this subject, for I was suddenly startled by hearing Oaklahoma Sam say, "This is Napoleon"; at the same time down went his knife over half an inch into the table. I had noticed from the first that Sam had scornfully pushed aside my table knife, preferring to use his own, although he had retained the use of my fork. Looking at once in that direction, I saw Tim's face turned my way, with sarcasm trembling on his lips, which only needed a little encouragement, and he would then utter one of his scathing sentences, thinking to blight at once the newly-opened flower of Sam's eloquence. "Don't look that way, look at me," cried the man from Oaklahoma, placing his left hand on Tim's shoulder, and speaking in a voice terribly quiet and firm. "I see," answered Tim, leaning back, with his two hands resting on the table—"I see; this is Napoleon." "Yes, and this is Blucher," continued Sam, taking the knife out of the table, and quickly planting it dangerously near to Tim's right hand. "And this," cried Sam, forcing his words between his teeth, and holding the knife suspended in the air, "is Wellington," and down it flashed between the two big fingers of Tim's left hand. Tim grew much paler as he removed that hand to his knee, and it was at once apparent to me that for the rest of the evening he was a spell-bound man, afraid to hazard even a civil question, for fear it would be misunderstood.

Next to Sam and Tim sat Chicago Slim, who was relating to Bony—an English beggar—his awful suffering for a week in the State of Utah, where a beggar had no other food than bread and milk confronting him on every threshold he approached, and how travelling in that part was known to all beggars as "the bread-and-milk route." Such were his awful sufferings, related to the sympathetic ears of Bony, who, in exchange, mentioned his own disappointments in England, "where," said he, "I find public-houses to be the easiest, quickest, and most profitable places." He was just about to cite instances when the Curly Kid, who had been listening to their conversation, asked Chicago Slim this question: "How is it that, when I was in Utah, the citizens did not baby me with bread and milk?" "Don't know," answered Slim, disconcerted not a little. "I went to no houses, but begged on the fly, and people had to give money or nothing. Slim, I reckon no true beggar would allow himself to be fed day after day on bread and milk." Chicago Slim did not answer, and at once fell in the estimation of Bony, who now considered him to be unworthy of further attention.

"I shall never forget," said Bony to the Curly Kid, who had by his remarks proved himself to be a beggar equal to any emergency—"I shall never forget my disgust when, one Sunday morning, I found myself accidentally in a town where public-houses are shut on the Sabbath day. I had to beg of proud, neatly-dressed church-goers, for the good-natured drinking man had not the heart to come out of doors, and you can imagine my ill success. How I wished all these people who were carrying Bibles and Prayer-books had bottles and jugs instead!"

How the hours passed, looking on these delightful companions! The first to leave was Tim, for Oaklahoma Sam had become personal about his rough beard, and wanted to shave him, there and then, with his knife; and, in fact, was sharpening it on a stone for that purpose, which I had often seen him do before. Tim civilly but firmly refused this kindness at Sam's hands, and, being afraid that he might be forced to undergo such an operation, got up, and saying "Good night, all," left the room.

Others followed, one by one, and two by two, until at last I was left alone with Brum. "Yes, and I must go too," said he; "for I intend to call on a dentist who is good for twenty-five cents." Saying which he also departed, leaving me standing alone, sad and motionless, at the end of the table.

"Here," said I, walking up the room, and looking affectionately at an empty chair—"here sat Wee Scotty; here sat Monkey Jim, and there sat Never Sweat; here sat Rags, and there sat Cinders; here sat Tim, and there sat Oaklahoma Sam." Indeed, there could be no mistake as to where Sam sat, for he had used his knife to such purpose, in describing the position of Napoleon, Blucher, and Wellington, and their rapid movements in the heat of battle, that the table-cloth was all in rags, and that part of the table was in splinters for nearly two feet square.

I stood undecided, for I had tasted their life, and I knew that it was after all far better than the chained life I was now leading. In an instant I made up my mind to follow Brum, and again enjoy the open-air camp fires, and saunterings in strange towns, and lying under shady trees in quiet woods, beside fresh springs. But I had scarcely moved when the room turned into a stone cell, and the wooden door became steel, and thick iron bars crossed the window. It must have been the strong feeling, incident to such a change, that made me wake.

I found myself sleeping alone in a small, poorly-furnished cottage, a stranger newly arrived in a strange village; and I had to admit, as a man in possession of all his senses, that I had far less cause to be happy than when I was a nameless wanderer with Brum in Louisiana, with Australian Red in Michigan, or cabined with Wee Scotty and Oaklahoma Sam on the cattleship Tritonia.

Chapter XXXVI

The Literary Life

One day, when I was small, my grandmother called me to her knee, and asked me if I knew where the White House was. No doubt I did, for I not only knew the town well, being a truant, but the green country for many a mile around. However, I did not know the house by name, and shook my head, at the same time looking at her with some anxiety, thinking that the White House was a place to whitewash the souls of wicked boys. Then she began to describe its beautiful situation, its numerous windows, the long drive through trees and the acres of green land that surrounded it. Did I know it now? I should think I did. It stood a long way back off a main road, and we truants often passed it. And we knew the apple orchard which belonged to that house, but was a long way from it; and it was less than a week before my grandmother asked this question, that I and a boy called "Trousers" had trespassed on the land, and filled our pockets and open shirts with red apples. So, when she continued talking about this house, I became a great deal confused, thinking that someone had been to her making enquiries of me; and I only had one thought to console me—"Trousers" was guilty also. My relief can be imagined when I found that such was not the case, but that my grandmother was thinking of her own days of childhood and, having no one else near, could not contain herself, but must make a confidant of a thoughtless boy, or—to use her own words—"a little black and a rodney." She was looking at the child that was dead in her, and could not feel me tremble at her knee, nor see my colour come and go. However, when I began to see that she knew nothing of my doings, and began to speak of her own childhood, I gradually became interested.

The White House, it seemed, had once belonged to a relative, and my grandmother had lived there for several months as a little girl. Now, my grandmother was an only child, and that she was allowed out of her mother's care for several months seemed strange. Perhaps it was owing to domestic strife. Her mother had married a worthless fellow who had at last drunk himself to death. So, I suppose she sent her only child away while she took steps to get rid of him and make a comfortable home of her own. Having a little property, and being a woman of great spirit, she ordered him out of the house and dared him to enter again. After which she started a small private school and, having the rent of four little houses, lived happy with her only child. No doubt she had come of good birth and was well educated. It was much against her wish that her daughter married my grandfather, in spite of his being captain of his own vessel—because of his want of education. Nevertheless, she lived to see her daughter married to an honest and affectionate man, even though his grammar was bad, and his roaring voice was not ashamed of it.

However, what interested me now was to hear from my grandmother that the lady at the White House had not only been very beautiful, but had been clever enough to write a book. As to her looks, my grandmother said that she and her husband made such a fine pair that even people that met them often turned and looked after them. They were both very tall, he being six feet three inches, and she being six feet; and they looked so stately that people made their admiration heard. My grandmother said that they were so fond of each other that they always walked arm-in-arm, as when lovers; and for this reason they were admired by those who would otherwise have frowned on their rich clothes and proud grace. But one day, when they had returned from riding, he, in assisting her from her horse, squeezed her breast, and this accident somehow caused her death. Such was my grandmother's account of former occupants of the White House. When I told these things to "Trousers," saying that we ought not to have robbed that orchard, he claimed that we had a right to the apples, because my grandmother used to live there. It was a great consolation to hear this, but still, I claimed the only right, and trusted that he would not lead others there on the sly.

But what I mean to say is this—the wonderful effect it had on me, young as I was, to hear that a relative of mine, however distant, had written a book! My feelings will be understood by all those who remember what books were to them as children. To children books do not reach millions, nor thousands; and when they have a book they think it is the first and last copy, and never dream that there are thousands more. It would be very hard to describe a child's opinion of a book, but there are thousands of grown people who are as innocent of the business side of literature, and who are still children in their knowledge of books. In fact, speaking of my own experience, I did not know until three or four years ago but what books must be published on their merit, and could not be published otherwise. I did not know, what I know so well now, that any person with money can publish a book, and that merit has little to do with it before publication, however much it may assist it after. Even now, speaking as the author of five books, I am still being surprised at the business side of literature. I find that books are pleasant things to brood on in an egg state, but that they are no sooner hatched and begin to move than they fill one with disgust and disappointment; and the author feels like the hen that without knowing hatched a brood of ducklings and, to her disgust, saw them run into the water.

Even in those early days I had made up my mind to write a book, so that it can be imagined what a sacred place the White House became to me. Day after day I thought of the lovely tall lady; and it was not her height, grace, or beauty, nor her wealth and social position that were uppermost in my thoughts—but that she had written a book! Time and again I asked my grandmother the name of it, but she could not tell. Of course I was too young to think of enquiring the author's name, and going to libraries, and trying to trace it that way. Very few grown people would have had sense enough for that.

Thinking of these things has led me to the contrast of literature as it seems to the young, and what it really is to a man of experience. You could never persuade a young man—and very few old men—that he could be one of the best writers of the day and yet starve, had he not the assistance of private means. "True," people say, "men of genius have starved, but the fault was that they were not recognized in their day." But the real truth is that a man may be so much recognized that the world's praise of his work would make a very large book indeed, and yet he may not have a second shirt to his back. It would be impossible to make people believe that a man could be so famous as to be invited to the houses of the great and yet be so shabby in appearance that beggars meet him on the road and, taking him for one of themselves, say, "Hallo! mate; what's yer luck?" And that when he did meet people of consequence, he had to sneak into back slums at night and sleep in a common lodging-house. People could not be made to believe any of these things while a man lives, but after he is dead they will believe anything.

Chapter XXXVII

The Sport of Fame

People have professed themselves amazed at my past life, and perhaps I can amaze them a little more by relating what great sport I and Fame have had; how she coaxed me into making several attempts to enrich the English language—some people think the attempts successful—and how she served me afterwards. Other people can be amazed at my past life, but my turn to be amazed comes now. The world has had its revenge for the few years I made it keep me as an idler.

In fact I have found Fame to be the most amusing companion I have ever had. She has placed me in such a position that I am now regarded as a liar, a miser, and a woman-hater. I am considered to be a liar by those who have read so much about my work, and who at last begin to doubt when I say that Fame in England does not pay so good as begging in America, and that a very small income of my own supports me. They cannot believe this to be possible after reading such noble accounts of my work—therefore I am a liar.

Again, I am regarded in the neighbourhood as a miser and a woman-hater because I do my own cooking, washing, and housework, when there are plenty of women around that would be glad of such work. Of course, these things are not done thoroughly and well, or I would have very little time to make attempts to enrich the English language. The truth of the matter is that they are so ill done, that I have had to write and stop several people from coming to interview me, because of spiders that often rope me to the ceiling, Jacky Longlegs that dance on my head, and—fleas. I am quite used to these things now, and take little notice of them, regarding them indeed as peculiar to the house of Fame.

Again, see what fun there must be when a man, grown famous, receives scores of letters, most of which address him as "Esquire"—"Esquire," mark you, and living in a three-shilling-a-week cottage! How his Majesty's proud servant in uniform must be amused at this, knowing that a man who lives in a cottage no larger than his cannot be of much consequence. He knows full well that innocent people far away mistake such a man for a fine gentleman, and he is apt to laugh at times, and in his serious moods to pity him. He has seen inside the cottage of this man, called "Esquire," and he saw nothing but bare walls and a few common things on the floor. If the poor man of genius said that he had enough praise to paper his walls, he would be laughed at for taking more pride in that than in a nice, comfortable home; and the idiot deserves to be laughed at, and to hang his head for shame.

Nothing worse could befall a living writer than to be compared to the mighty dead. It is most certainly a great compliment, and a great help to a man's spirit, but the consequence is apt to be fatal to his flesh. The mistake is that people are likely to think of him as one dead, and, of course, dead men need no food, clothing, or rent. Being regarded as one dead, he is naturally not thought of when there is anything given away; and the vast multitudes of powerful English people who are so eager to reward struggling genius—foreign or native—must, in consequence, overlook a man so highly rated.

All this is quite natural, but it is very amusing. It is very amusing to receive by post a request for one's autograph when one is in the act of washing a dirty pair of stockings, and lucky to have them to wash.

In spite of leading a lonely life, I do not often talk or laugh aloud, but I did on this occasion. It was that merry kind of laugh a man makes when he has just had a letter to say that he is ruined and a beggar, and while he is in the act of reading it his wife comes into the room and says, "George, I want ten pounds for a new dress." He has read the letter, and he has heard his wife's words, and he shrieks with merry laughter—as I did.

I know well that a man of genius has shivered on a winter's night, in a bed with insufficient clothing, in spite of using all his wearing apparel, after having received that day a noble tribute from the press, in which a well-known critic said he was unrivalled by his contemporaries. That he lay all night shivering with the cold, and expected to be poor Cock Robin before morning.

True, a man's first book of poetry may run into a second edition, but people should not write and congratulate him on his success before they know what that means. He may have received a cheque that never mentioned pounds, only shillings and pennies, and perhaps far more pennies than shillings. Of course, these are the impish tricks of Fame, and people can hardly be blamed.

But the innocence of this world has often annoyed and surprised me. A man, who knew my circumstances thoroughly, was so little astonished to know how I could buy provisions, coal, oil, wood, clothes, boots, etc. etc. etc., and to also answer a kind world's forced correspondence—he, I say, was so little amazed to know how all these things could be done on a paltry few shillings a week, that he suggested it would save me much time and trouble to hire a woman once a week to clean the place; and that it would only cost two or three shillings; I did not answer him, for I was very much afraid of having one of those merry laughing fits that have come on me so often since I have been the companion of Fame.

I shall never forget the day when I was compared to the great Daniel Defoe. At that time I could not spare money for a pair of stockings, so I tore an old shirt in strips and wound them round my feet, as tramps often do. Several times I noticed that people glanced down at the feet of the second Daniel Defoe, but I could not think how they could possibly know of my self-made stockings. In fact Fame was having such sport with me on this occasion that I had forgotten all about them. The name of Daniel Defoe had had a wonderful effect on me; it had put fire under my feet, and a steel rod in my back.

While I was marching along in this stiff frame of pride, a little girl came running forward, and said, "Please, sir, you've dropped something." Looking on the ground I saw, to my amazement, that one of the toe-rags, which had unwound itself, was lying in sight, but still attached to my boot. But what amused me more was to think that it had been trailing on the ground for a considerable time, and that I had passed several ladies; and one of them I was beginning to be interested in, for she had often looked at me as if she knew I was famous. This is only one of the many funny little things that have happened since I have been compared in England to the mighty dead, and you can imagine my laughter.

The following day a great literary paper praised my work, and said that it deserved its success, and that no man would envy such a writer a four-storey mansion in the West End. Alas! a few days after this I received a letter to congratulate me on my success, which made special mention of my four-storey mansion; whereas at the same time I was living in a small cottage with no more furniture than a little boy could lift, and a friend was paying my rent.

Of course, we know very well that nothing can be done for genius. Unfortunately, Nature does not mark him at birth, or we could soon put an end to him; and not only save the State worry, but, better still, save him from the cruel sport of Fame. If we give him twenty pounds, what will he do with it? Will he open a fish shop or buy a milk round? Not he; he has not the sense to do anything of the kind. The idiot will buy books, and idle his time away at writing, and his twenty pounds is soon gone, and the money is wasted. "But if he enriches the English language?" one suggests. Ha! ha! tell that nonsense to an Organized Charity, and hear their opinion. No, he had his chance to open a fish shop and make a living, but he sat down and idled his time away at writing.

For all that we cannot allow this poor wretch to suffer; but what, in the name of goodness, can we do? I suggest this: no sooner is a man acclaimed as a genius, and compared to the mightiest dead, than the State should at once supply him with a distinguishing uniform; so that he would not only be sure of clothes, but would also be able to command the respect of strangers, however humble his circumstances are. Not only that, but the vast multitudes of powerful English people who are so eager to reward genius would then have an opportunity to recognize him in the street, and assist him with cheques, bank-notes, etc.; which the man of genius—poet, painter, musician, no matter what—could take with dignity, as his due, and not be expected to demean himself by a great show of thanks. All he would then have to do would be to walk abroad, and give his address to such rich people as accosted him, so that they could send to his house food ready cooked, clean bed-clothes, money for rent, and other things.

Chapter XXXVIII

Beggars in the Making

I often feel upset to think that these articles on begging may rob honest men of charity; that people will become under the impression that beggars are born instead of made; aye, even born full-fledged, without having had childhood or youth. I would not like people to think that every man that knocks at their door is a professional tramp; or every voice they hear singing in the street is that of an impostor. It must be confessed that the latter is very probably one, seeing that a man either has to be on the road a long time before he takes courage to sing in public, or must be under the influence of drink. I have seen in provincial towns as many as four men singing together. In a case of this kind, they are almost sure to be real out-of-works, and the reason they sing instead of beg houses is that they cannot all four go to one house, and individually they lack courage; but they can sing all together, each one getting courage from the presence of his companions.

People never give it a thought how difficult it is for a stranger to get work, even where there is work in abundance. In new countries things are different; a man is hired at once, without a question of name and address. But in our old countries masters will not hire strange tramps, until they are at the last extremity. I have seen, this last summer, almost within a stone's throw of me, a farmer let his hay be spoilt by the rain, through having insufficient labour, and refusing to employ one or two of the many poor fellows that came looking for work. He, and the few men he had, worked day and night, rather than he would hire a stranger. No doubt he expected Providence to withhold the rain for his sake, and she, kind soul, gave him more than two weeks happy sunshine, quite sufficient if he had not been too greedy to do as much work as possible himself, and pay away little to others. So the rain came, and he suffered in consequence. If people knew the number of men of this kind there are in the land, they would not be so hasty in telling tramps that the farmers are busy with their harvest, and are in sad need of men.

Although I have met several men and women that could claim to being born beggars, having been born of beggars on the road, yet for all that, people must not think that this is quite common. One time I met one of these in Bedfordshire, and he recommended me to a good row of houses, which he advised me to call at that evening. What this man did not know about begging was not much. After doing business in several streets, and finding trade very quiet indeed, I made up my mind to call at that row of small cottages on my way back to the lodging-house. It was then almost dark, being winter, and I could not well make out my surroundings. However, I went the whole length of the row, and was only refused at one cottage. Two of them gave pennies, one gave a halfpenny, one gave three farthings, and two gave food. This was certainly not bad, in so short a time, and from such humble dwellings, and considering the ill-luck I had had at rows and rows of fine villas. That night, when I was in the lodging-house kitchen, my born beggar asked me if I had called at the cottages, and, if so, how they had treated me. "Splendid," I answered, with a smile of gratitude, for it is not often that a beggar will give information of this kind to a stranger. "The almshouses are always good," he said, in a whisper. "Almshouses!" I ejaculated, with astonishment, and a good deal of annoyance. "Yes; you will always find them good," he continued, with the utmost unconcern, and beginning to whistle a popular tune. This man was a born beggar, without the least shame.

But men of this kind are rare, and people must not forget that the man who stands before them has gone through the various stages—from a respectable working man with a home, to a man without employment, who is looking for work; one that must either beg or starve, who has wandered from his native town, where his friends are, to places where cruel Rumour has said abundant work is to be had. For three or four months he is an honest seeker of work, but after that despair makes him indifferent. He gets disappointed so many times, running here and there, at the recommendation of people that would do him a kindness, and others that tell him lies to get rid of him—he gets disappointed so often that in a short while he will not go out of his way at all, although he says that he will do so. He soon begins to see that there is not very great difficulty in getting enough to eat and a few coppers for his lodging, and, of course, the consequence is that he soon becomes contented with a beggar's lot. It will not be long after this change of feeling that he will be heard to say in a lodging-house kitchen, while he is drinking hot tea and eating fresh toast—"Who's looking for work, eh? Not me!" But people must remember that this man may come to beg them when he is in the first stage, and desirous of work, and is therefore a well-deserving man.

The fact of the matter is that no outsider can tell a beggar from an honest seeker of work. A woman gives a man charity because he talks nice and approaches her in a respectable manner; and she believes him at once when he says that he has only been out of work six weeks. The dear lady cannot see that he has not a thing on his body that was bought by himself. His boots are two sizes too large, and have turned up at the toes; his coat is too short, and his waistcoat is too long; his trousers were made for a fat man; not to mention a shirt that either cannot be buttoned at the collar, or could be buttoned around two necks like his. Even if the lady or gentleman noted these things, they could not read any tales in them, and it would never occur to them to try to do so. Now, seeing that this man is so ill-fitted, it plainly shows that all his things are begged; and seeing that clothes last a man a considerable time, and that this beggar has nothing of his own, is sufficient proof that he must have been on the road six months at the least.

Of course, there have been cases of men starting on the road with good clothes and boots, which they had to sell almost at once for food and lodging at a second-hand shop. The dealer that buys must give these men substitutes to cover their nakedness, and these old things would be hardly likely to fit well.

This would account for the strange appearance of a few men, but very few; for when men start on the road they are so full of confidence in getting work soon that they do not dress in clothes good enough to sell, but leave them at home, or in their lodgings, to be sent for when they are settled.

One way to tell a beggar who has been on the road a long time is to employ the slang of the road, which few people can do. When a beggar came to my door the other day, he first asked for a drink of water. I gave him this, and had a penny ready in my hand to give him when he returned the glass. I may as well say here that I never refuse these men a penny, poor as I am, and whatever he is to my judgment. If I think he is a working man, he gets the penny out of pity and sympathy; and, if I judge him to be a real beggar, I give it to him out of admiration. However, this man drank the water and then—not to my surprise—asked for a mouthful of something to eat. With a smile I gave him the penny and prepared to shut the door. But this man was a true beggar, for getting a penny so easy, without having to talk for it, emboldened him; so he began in a ready voice to lament his old clothes, and to ask me if I could assist him with others. "Look here," I said, with deliberation, and looking him straight in the face—"Look here, matey; if I could patter as good as you I'd go on the toe-be to-morrow." For a moment he seemed taken by surprise, and then he drew his hand down over his face, in an attempt to wipe out a smile; but it was of no use, for the next moment he stood grinning from ear to ear. "I see you know the biz, gov'nor," he said, going away; "but you know very well that sixteen farthings for the feather takes some getting."

W.H. Davies – A Short Biography

William Henry Davies, but always known as W. H. Davies, was born at 6, Portland Street in the Pillgwenlly district of Newport, Monmouthshire, Wales, a busy port on July 3rd, 1871.

In November 1874, when he was three, his father, an iron moulder, died. The following year his mother, Mary Anne Davies, remarried to become Mrs Joseph Hill. She agreed that the three children should pass into the care of the paternal grandparents, Francis and Lydia Davies, who ran the nearby Church House Inn at 14, Portland Street.

Davies seemed to find childhood difficult. By the age of 13 he was arrested, part of a gang of five schoolmates, and charged with stealing handbags. He was given twelve strokes of the birch. The following year, 1885, Davies wrote his first poem; "Death".

However, he did have an appetite for reading and as he later recounted, at the age of 14, when left to sit with his dying grandfather that he missed the moment of his grandfather's passing as he was too engrossed in reading "a very interesting book of wild adventure".

In November 1886 with his schooling finished he began a five-year apprenticeship to a local picture-frame maker. He never settled at this craft or indeed any regular work. His yearning was to travel. Davies was apparently a difficult and somewhat delinquent young man, and made many requests to his grandmother to lend him funds so that he could sail to America. Eventually in 1893 through his own resources he reached America. In a half dozen years, he crossed the Atlantic at least annually by working on cattle ships. He travelled through many of the states, sometimes begging, sometimes taking seasonal work, but would often spend any savings on a drinking spree with a fellow traveller.

His turning point arrived when, after a week of rambling in London, he came across a newspaper story about the riches to be made in the Klondike and immediately set off to make his fortune in Canada. Attempting to jump a freight train at Renfrew, Ontario, on March 20th, 1899, with fellow tramp Three-fingered Jack, he lost his footing and his right foot was crushed under the wheels of the train. The leg later had to be amputated below the knee and he wore a wooden prosthetic leg thereafter.

Davies later wrote: "I bore this accident with an outward fortitude that was far from the true state of my feelings. Thinking of my present helplessness caused me many a bitter moment, but I managed to impress all comers with a false indifference ... I was soon home again, having been away less than four months; but all the wildness had been taken out of me, and my adventures after this were not of my own seeking, but the result of circumstances."

He returned to Britain, living a rough life in London shelters and doss-houses. Unsure of the possible reaction from his fellow tramps to his poetry, he would often feign sleep as he mentally composed his poems for later commitment to paper. At one stage he borrowed money to have his poems printed on loose sheets of paper, which he then tried to sell door-to-door through the streets of residential London. The enterprise failed.

Davies published his first book of poetry, The Soul's Destroyer, in 1905, again by means of his own savings. By cutting back expenditure to almost nothing and living the life of a tramp for six months (with the first draft of the book hidden in his pocket), and a small loan of funds from his inheritance it was eventually published. The volume was largely ignored and he took to posting copies to prospective wealthy customers taken from the pages of Who's Who, and asking them to send a half crown, in return. He eventually managed to sell 60 of the 200 copies printed.

One of the copies was sent to Arthur Adcock, a journalist with the Daily Mail. Adcock later wrote in his essay "Gods of Modern Grub Street", that he "recognised that there were crudities and even doggerel in it, there was also in it some of the freshest and most magical poetry to be found in modern books". He sent the half crown and asked Davies to meet him. Adcock is still regarded as "the man who discovered Davies". The first trade edition of The Soul's Destroyer was published in 1907. Further editions followed in 1908 and 1910.

On October 12th, 1905 Davies met the poet Edward Thomas, then literary critic for the Daily Chronicle. Thomas rented for Davies the tiny two-roomed "Stidulph's Cottage", in Egg Pie Lane, in the second week of February 1907. The cottage was "only two meadows off" from Thomas' own house. Thomas adopted the role of protective guardian for Davies, on one occasion even arranging for the manufacture, by a local wheelwright, of a replacement wooden leg. Thomas also made every effort to promote Davis's talent into a meaningful career.

In 1907, the manuscript of The Autobiography of a Super-Tramp drew the attention of George Bernard Shaw, who agreed to write a preface. It was because of Shaw that Davies' contract with the publishers was rewritten to allow the author to retain the serial rights, reversion of all rights after three years, royalties of fifteen per cent of selling price and a non-returnable advance of twenty-five pounds. He was also to have a say on the style of illustrations, advertisement layouts and cover designs. The original publisher, Duckworth and Sons, refused these demands and the book was released instead by Fifield.

In 1911, Davies was awarded a Civil List Pension of £50, which later increased to £100 and then to £150.

In London Davies started to spend more time in literary circles, even starting an autograph collection. The influential Georgian poetry publisher, Edward Marsh, introduced Davies to DH Lawrence and his wife Frieda in July, 1913 and Davies was able to secure an autograph from DH Lawrence

Lawrence was captivated by Davies and later invited him to join them in Germany. Despite this early enthusiasm Lawrence's opinion waned after reading Foliage and further after reading Nature Poems he noted that the verses seemed "so thin, one can hardly feel them".

After several temporary abodes, Davies, in early 1914, rented rooms at 14 Great Russell Street, previously the residence of Charles Dickens in London's Bloomsbury district. Here in a two-room apartment, infested with mice and rats, and next door to a noisy Belgian prostitute, he lived from early 1916 until 1921. Davies now expanded his career by giving a series of public readings of his work, alongside others such as Hilaire Belloc and W. B. Yeats and also impressed his fellow poet Ezra Pound.

Davies was always a person of some fascination by fellow artists. His head was cast in bronze in 1916 by the famed sculptor Jacob Epstein's works.

He enjoyed the company of literary men and their conversation, particularly in the rarefied atmosphere of the Café Royal. Another haunt was the Mont Blanc in Soho and with it the company of W. H. Hudson, Edward Garrett and others.

In the last months of 1921, Davies moved to Brook Street to rent rooms from the Quaker poet Olaf Baker. He began to find prolonged work difficult, however, suffering from increased bouts of rheumatism and other ailments.

On February 5th, 1923, he married 23-year-old Helen Matilda Payne, at the Registry Office in East Grinstead in Sussex. His book Young Emma chronicles the relationship in a very frank and revealing way. Having second thoughts he retrieved the book from the publishers and it was only published after Helens death several decades later. He had met her near Marble Arch decanting from a bus wearing a "saucy-looking little velvet cap with tassels". At the time Helen was unmarried and pregnant. Whilst living with Davies in London, before the couple were married, Helen suffered an almost fatal miscarriage.

The couple lived quietly and happily, moving first to Sevenoaks, then to "Malpas House", Oxted in Surrey and finally moving through a series of five different residences at Nailsworth in Gloucestershire. The couple had no children.

Davies was always keen to find different modes to express his work. He made over a dozen broadcasts for the BBC, reading his own work, between 1924 and 1940.

In 1925, a further volume of auto-biography, Later Days, describes the beginnings of Davies' career as a writer and his acquaintance with Hilaire Belloc, George Bernard Shaw and Walter de la Mare, amongst many others.

By now his reputation had also made him "the most painted literary man of his day", drawn and painted by many including Augustus John.

In 1930 he edited the poetry anthology Jewels of Song for Cape, choosing works by more than 120 different poets, and including William Blake, Thomas Campion, William Shakespeare, Alfred, Lord Tennyson and W. B. Yeats. Of his own poems he selected only "The Kingfisher" and "Leisure".

Davies returned to Newport, in September 1938, for the unveiling of a plaque in his honour at the Church House Inn. An address was given by the Poet Laureate John Masefield. He was still unwell, however, and this proved to be his last public appearance.

About three months before he died, Davies was visited at Glendower by Gordon Woodhouse and the Sitwells, Davies being too ill to travel to dinner at Nether Lypiatt. Osbert Sitwell noted that Davies looked "very ill" but that "…. his head, so typical of him in its rustic and nautical boldness, with the black hair now greying a little, but as stiff as ever, surrounding his high bony forehead, seemed to have acquired an even more sculptural quality." Helen privately explained to Sitwell that Davies' heart showed "alarming symptoms of weakness" caused, according to his doctors, by the dragging weight of his wooden leg. Helen had been careful to keep the true extent of the medical diagnosis from her husband.

Davies himself confided in Sitwell: "I've never been ill before, really, except when I had that accident and lost my leg … And, d'you know, I grow so irritable when I've got that pain, I can't bear the sound of people's voices. … Sometimes I feel I should like to turn over on my side and die."

W. H. Davies' health continued to deteriorate and he died, on September 26th, 1940, at the age of 69.

W. H. Davies – A Concise Bibliography

The Soul's Destroyer and Other Poems (of the author, The Farmhouse, 1905) (also Alston Rivers, 1907), New Poems, 1907
Nature Poems, 1908
The Autobiography of a Super-Tramp, 1908
How It Feels To Be Out of Work (The English Review, 1 Dec 1908)
Beggars, 1909
Farewell to Poesy, 1910
Songs of Joy and Others, 1911
A Weak Woman, 1911
The True Traveller, 1912
Foliage: Various Poems,
Nature, 1914
The Bird of Paradise,
Child Lovers,
Collected Poems,
A Poet's Pilgrimage (or A Pilgrimage In Wales), 1918
Forty New Poems, 1918
Raptures, 1918
The Song of Life, 1920
The Captive Lion and Other Poems, 1921
Form (Editor Davies and Austin O Spare), Vol 1, Numbers 1, 2 & 3, 1921/1922

The Hour of Magic, 1922
Shorter Lyrics of the Twentieth Century, 1900–1922. Editor Davies, 1922
True Travellers. A Tramp's Opera in Three Acts, 1923
Collected Poems, 1st Series, 1923
Collected Poems, 2nd Series, 1923
Selected Poems, 1923
'Poets and Critics' - New Statesman, 21, Sept 8th 1923
What I Gained and Lost By Not Staying At School. Teachers World 29, June 1923
Secrets, 1924
Moll Flanders. Introduction by Davies, 1924
A Poet's Alphabet, 1925
Later Days, 1925
Augustan Book of Poetry: Thirty Selected Poems,
The Song of Love, 1926
The Adventures of Johnny Walker, 1926
A Poet's Calendar, 1927
Dancing Mad, 1927
The Collected Poems of W. H. Davies, 1928
Moss and Feather, 1928
Forty Nine Poems, 1928
Selected Poems, Arranged by Edward Garnett, introduction by Davies, 1928
Ambition and Other Poems, 1929
Jewels of Song (Editor. Anthology, 1930
In Winter, 1931
Poems 1930–31, 1931
The Lover's Song Book, 1933
My Birds, 1933
My Garden, 1933
'Memories' - School, 1, Nov 1933
The Poems of W. H. Davies: A Complete Collection, 1934
Love Poems, 1935
The Birth of Song, 1936
'Epilogue' to The Romance of the Echoing Wood, 1937
An Anthology of Short Poems (Editor. Anthology, 1938
The Loneliest Mountain, 1939
The Poems of W. H. Davies, 1940
Common Joys and Other Poems, 1941
Collected Poems of W. H. Davies, 1943

www.ingramcontent.com/pod-product-compliance
Lightning Source LLC
Chambersburg PA
CBHW060139050426
42448CB00010B/2203